Gary Ives
Editor

Electronic Journal Management Systems: Experiences from the Field

Electronic Journal Management Systems: Experiences from the Field has been co-published simultaneously as *The Serials Librarian*, Volume 47, Number 4 2005.

Pre-publication REVIEWS, COMMENTARIES, EVALUATIONS . . .

"A valuable addition to the professional development collection of every academic library. Solutions to the challenges of 'back office' management of electronic subscriptions, as well as solutions for facilitating and streamlining access for library patrons, are described."

Anne Prestamo, EdD, MLIS, BM
Associate Dean for Collection and Technology Services
Oklahoma State University Libraries

The Haworth Information Press®
An Imprint of The Haworth Press, Inc.

Electronic Journal Management Systems: Experiences from the Field

Electronic Journal Management Systems: Experiences from the Field has been co-published simultaneously as *The Serials Librarian*, Volume 47, Number 4 2005.

Monographic Separates from *The Serials Librarian*

For additional information on these and other Haworth Press titles, including descriptions, tables of contents, reviews, and prices, use the QuickSearch catalog at http://www.HaworthPress.com.

Electronic Journal Management Systems: Experiences from the Field, edited by Gary Ives, MLS (Vol. 47, No. 4, 2005). *"A valuable addition to the professional development collection of every academic library. Solutions to the challenges of 'back office' management of electronic subscriptions, as well as solutions for facilitating and streamlining access for library patrons, are described."* (Anne Prestamo, EdD, MLIS, BM, Associate Dean for Collection and Technology Services, Oklahoma State University Libraries)

E-Serials Cataloging: Access to Continuing and Integrating Resources via the Catalog and the Web, edited by Jim Cole, MA, and Wayne Jones, MA, MLS (Vol. 41, No. 3/4, 2002). *"A very timely and useful reference tool for librarians. The best . . . on various aspects of e-serials: from standards to education and training, from policies and procedures to national and local projects and future trends. As a technical services librarian, I found the sections on policies and procedures and national projects and local applications very valuable and informative."* (Vinh-The Lam, MLS, Head, Cataloging Department, University of Saskatchewan Library, Canada)

Women's Studies Serials: A Quarter-Century of Development, edited by Kristin H. Gerhard, MLS (Vol. 35, No. 1/2, 1998). *"Candidly explores and analyzes issues which must be addressed to ensure the continued growth and vitality of women's studies. . . . It commands the attention of librarians, scholars, and publishers."* (Joan Ariel, MLS, MA, Women's Studies Librarian and Lecturer, University of California at Irvine)

E-Serials: Publishers, Libraries, Users, and Standards, edited by Wayne Jones, MA, MLS (Vol. 33, No. 1/2/3/4, 1998). *"Libraries and publishers will find this book helpful in developing strategies, policies, and procedures."* (Nancy Brodie, National Library of Canada, Ottawa, Ontario)

Serials Cataloging at the Turn of the Century, edited by Jeanne M. K. Boydston, MSLIS, James W. Williams, MSLS, and Jim Cole, MLS (Vol. 32, No. 1/2, 1997). *Focuses on the currently evolving trends in serials cataloging in order to predict and explore the possibilities for the field in the new millennium.*

Serials Management in the Electronic Era: Papers in Honor of Peter Gellatly, Founding Editor of The Serials Librarian, edited by Jim Cole, MA, and James W. Williams, MLS (Vol. 29, No. 3/4, 1996). *Assesses progress and technical changes in the field of serials management and anticipates future directions and challenges for librarians.*

Special Format Serials and Issues: Annual Review of . . . , Advances in . . . , Symposia on . . . , Methods in . . . , by Tony Stankus, MLS (Vol. 27, No. 2/3, 1996). *A thorough and lively introduction to the nature of these publications' types.*

Serials Canada: Aspects of Serials Work in Canadian Libraries, edited by Wayne Jones, MLS (Vol. 26, No. 3/4, 1996). *"An excellent addition to the library literature and is recommended for all library school libraries, scholars, and students of comparative/international librarianship."* (Library Times International)

Serials Cataloging: Modern Perspectives and International Developments, edited by Jim E. Cole, MA, and James W. Williams, MSLS (Vol. 22, No. 1/2/3/4, 1993). *"A significant contribution to understanding the 'big picture' of serials control. . . . A solid presentation of serious issues in a crucial area on librarianship."* (Bimonthly Review of Law Books)

Making Sense of Journals in the Life Sciences: From Specialty Origins to Contemporary Assortment, by Tony Stankus (Supp. #08, 1992, 1996). *"An excellent introduction to scientific periodical literature and the disciplines it serves."* (College & Research Libraries News)

Making Sense of Journals in the Physical Sciences: From Specialty Origins to Contemporary Assortment, by Tony Stankus, MLS (Supp. #07, 1992, 1996). *"A tour de force . . . It will immeasurably help science serials librarians to select journal titles on a rational and defensible basis, and the methodology used can be extended over time and to other fields and other journals."* (International Journal of Information and Library Research)

The North American Serials Interest Group (NASIG) Series

Serials in the Park, edited by Patricia Sheldahl French and Richard Worthing (Vol. 46, No. 1/2/3/4, 2004). *Proceedings of the 18th Annual NASIG conference (2003, Portland, Oregon), focusing on the most significant trends and innovations for serials.*

Transforming Serials: The Revolution Continues, edited by Susan L. Scheiberg and Shelley Neville (Vol. 44, No. 1/2/3/4, 2003). *"A valuable and thought-provoking resource for all library workers involved with serials." (Mary Curran, MLS, MA, Head of Cataloguing Services, University of Ottawa, Ontario, Canada)*

NASIG 2001: A Serials Odyssey, edited by Susan L. Scheiberg and Shelley Neville (Vol. 42, No. 1/2/3/4, 2002). *From XML to ONIX and UCITA, here's cutting-edge information from leading serials librarians from the 16th NASIG conference.*

Making Waves: New Serials Landscapes in a Sea of Change, edited by Joseph C. Harmon and P. Michelle Fiander (Vol. 40, No. 1/2/3/4, 2001). *These proceedings include discussions of the Digital Millennium Copyright Act, and reports on specific test projects such as BioOne, the Open Archives Project, and PubMed Central.*

From Carnegie to Internet 2: Forging the Serials Future, edited by P. Michelle Fiander, Joseph C. Harmon, and Jonathan David Makepeace (Vol. 38, No. 1/2/3/4, 2000). *Current information and practical insight to help you improve your technical skills and prepare you and your library for the 21st century.*

Head in the Clouds, Feet on the Ground: Serials Vision and Common Sense, edited by Jeffrey S. Bullington, Beatrice L. Caraway, and Beverley Geer (Vol. 36, No. 1/2/3/4, 1999). *"Practical, common sense advice, and visionary solutions to serials issues afoot in every library department and in every type of library today. . . . An essential reference guide for libraries embracing electronic resource access." (Mary Curran, MA, MLS, Coordinator, Bibliographic Standards, Morisset Library, University of Ottawa, Ontario, Canada)*

Experimentation and Collaboration: Creating Serials for a New Millennium, Charlene N. Simser and Michael A. Somers (Vol. 34, No. 1/2/3/4, 1998). *Gives valuable ideas and practical advice that you can apply or incorporate into your own area of expertise.*

Pioneering New Serials Frontiers: From Petroglyphs to Cyberserials, edited by Christine Christiansen and Cecilia Leathem (Vol. 30, No. 3/4, and Vol. 31, No. 1/2, 1997). *Gives you insight, ideas, and practical skills for dealing with the changing world of serials management.*

Serials to the Tenth Power: Traditions, Technology, and Transformation, edited by Mary Ann Sheble, MLS, and Beth Holley, MLS (Vol. 28, No. 1/2/3/4, 1996). *Provides readers with practical ideas on managing the challenges of the electronic information environment.*

A Kaleidoscope of Choices: Reshaping Roles and Opportunities for Serialists, edited by Beth Holley, MLS, and Mary Ann Sheble, MLS (Vol. 25, No. 3/4, 1995). *"Highly recommended as an excellent source material for all librarians interested in learning more about the Internet, technology and its effect on library organization and operations, and the virtual library." (Library Acquisitions: Practice & Theory)*

New Scholarship: New Serials: Proceedings of the North American Serials Interest Group, Inc., edited by Gail McMillan and Marilyn Norstedt (Vol. 24, No. 3/4, 1994). *"An excellent representation of the ever-changing, complicated, and exciting world of serials." (Library Acquisitions Practice & Theory)*

If We Build It: Scholarly Communications and Networking Technologies: Proceedings of the North American Serials Interest Group, Inc., edited by Suzanne McMahon, MLS, Miriam Palm, MLS, and Pamela Dunn, BA (Vol. 23, No. 3/4, 1993). *"Highly recommended to anyone interested in the academic serials environment as a means of keeping track of the electronic revolution and the new possibilities emerging." (ASL (Australian Special Libraries))*

A Changing World: Proceedings of the North American Serials Interest Group, Inc., edited by Suzanne McMahon, MLS, Miriam Palm, MLS, and Pamela Dunn, BA (Vol. 21, No. 2/3, 1992). *"A worthy publication for anyone interested in the current and future trends of serials control and electronic publishing." (Library Resources & Technical Services)*

Published by

The Haworth Information Press®, 10 Alice Street, Binghamton, NY 13904-1580 USA

The Haworth Information Press® is an imprint of The Haworth Press, Inc., 10 Alice Street, Binghamton, NY 13904-1580 USA.

Electronic Journal Management Systems: Experiences from the Field has been co-published simultaneously as *The Serials Librarian*, Volume 47, Number 4 2005.

The development, preparation, and publication of this work has been undertaken with great care. However, the publisher, employees, editors, and agents of The Haworth Press and all imprints of The Haworth Press, Inc., including The Haworth Medical Press® and Pharmaceutical Products Press®, are not responsible for any errors contained herein or for consequences that may ensue from use of materials or information contained in this work. Opinions expressed by the author(s) are not necessarily those of The Haworth Press, Inc. With regard to case studies, identities and circumstances of individuals discussed herein have been changed to protect confidentiality. Any resemblance to actual persons, living or dead, is entirely coincidental.

Cover design by Jennifer M. Gaska

Ives, Gary.
    Electronic journal management systems : experiences from the field / Gary Ives.
        p. cm.
    Simultaneously published as The serials librarian, v. 47, no. 4, 2005.
    Includes bibliographical references and index.
    ISBN-13: 978-0-7890-2595-1 (hard cover : alk. paper)
    ISBN-10: 0-7890-2595-7 (hard cover : alk. paper)
    ISBN-13: 978-0-7890-2596-8 (soft cover : alk. paper)
    ISBN-10: 0-7890-2596-5 (soft cover : alk. paper)
    1. Libraries–Special collections–Electronic journals. 2. Serials control systems. 3. Electronic journals–United States–Management–Case studies. I. Serials librarian. II. Title.

    Z692.E43195 2005
    025.2'84–dc22
                                                                          2004027876

Electronic Journal Management Systems: Experiences from the Field

Gary Ives
Editor

Electronic Journal Management Systems: Experiences from the Field has been co-published simultaneously as *The Serials Librarian*, Volume 47, Number 4 2005.

The Haworth Information Press®
An Imprint of The Haworth Press, Inc.

New York • London • Victoria (AU)
www.HaworthPress.com

∞ ALL HAWORTH INFORMATION PRESS
    BOOKS AND JOURNALS ARE PRINTED
    ON CERTIFIED ACID-FREE PAPER

Indexing, Abstracting & Website/Internet Coverage

The Serials Librarian

This section provides you with a list of major indexing & abstracting services and other tools for bibliographic access. That is to say, each service began covering this periodical during the year noted in the right column. Most Websites which are listed below have indicated that they will either post, disseminate, compile, archive, cite or alert their own Website users with research-based content from this work. (This list is as current as the copyright date of this publication.)

Abstracting, Website/Indexing Coverage . . . . Year When Coverage Began

- *Academic Abstracts/CD-ROM* **1993**
- *Academic Search: Database of 2,000 selected academic serials, updated monthly: EBSCO Publishing* **1993**
- *Academic Search Elite (EBSCO)* **1993**
- *Business Source Corporate: Coverage of nearly 3,350 quality magazines and journals; designed to meet the diverse information needs of corporations; EBSCO Publishing <http://www.epnet.com/corporate/bsourcecorp.asp>* **1993**
- *CareData: the database supporting social care management and practice <http://www.elsc.org.uk/caredata/caredata.htm>* . . . **2003**
- *Chemical Abstracts Service–monitors, indexes & abstracts the world's chemical literature, updates this information daily, and makes it accessible through state-of-the-art information services <http://www.cas.org>* **1982**
- *CINAHL (Cumulative Index to Nursing & Allied Health Literature), in print, EBSCO, and SilverPlatter, DataStar, and PaperChase. (Support materials include Subject Heading List, Database Search Guide, and instructional video.) <http://www.cinahl.com>* **1985**
- *Computer and Information Systems Abstracts <http://www.csa.com>* . . . **2004**

(continued)

- *Current Cites [Digital Libraries] [Electronic Publishing] [Multimedia & Hypermedia] [Networks & Networking] [General] <http://sunsite.berkeley.edu/CurrentCites/>* 2000
- *Current Index to Journals in Education* 2001
- *EBSCOhost Electronic Journals Service (EJS) <http://ejournals.ebsco.com>* 2001
- *Foods Adlibra* .... *
- *FRANCIS.INIST/CNRS <http://www.inist.fr>* 1992
- *Google <http://www.google.com>* 2004
- *Google Scholar <http://scholar.google.com>* 2004
- *Handbook of Latin American Studies* 1992
- *Haworth Document Delivery Center* 1976
- *Hein's Legal Periodical Checklist: Index to Periodical Articles Pertaining to Law <http://www.wshein.com>* 1989
- *IBZ International Bibliography of Periodical Literature <http://www.saur.de>* 1993
- *Index Guide to College Journals (core list compiled by integrating 48 indexes frequently used to support undergraduate programs in small to medium sized libraries)* 1999
- *Index to Periodical Articles Related to Law <http://www.law.utexas.edu>* 1990
- *Information Reports & Bibliographies* 1992
- *Information Sciences & Technology Abstracts: indexes journal articles from more than 450 publications as well as books, research reports, and conference proceedings; EBSCO Publishing <http://www.epnet.com>* 1970
- *Informed Librarian, The <http://www.informedlibrarian.com>* 1993
- *INSPEC is the leading English-language bibliographic service providing access to the world's scientific & technical literature in physics, electrical engineering, electronics, communications, control engineering, computers & computing, and information technology <http://www.iee.org.uk/publish/>* 2002
- *Internationale Bibliographie der geistes- und sozialwissenschaftlichen Zeitschriftenliteratur ... See IBZ <http://www.saur.de>* 1993
- *Journal of Academic Librarianship: Guide to Professional Literature, The* 1992
- *Konyvtari Figyelo (Library Review)* 1995
- *Library & Information Science Abstracts (LISA) <http://www.csa.com>* .. 1990
- *Library and Information Science Annual (LISCA) <http://www.lu.com>* 1997

(continued)

- *Library Literature & Information Science*
  <http://www.hwwilson.com> **1989**
- *Linguistics & Language Behavior Abstracts (LLBA)*
  <http://www.csa.com> **1996**
- *Magazines for Libraries (Katz) . . . (see 2003 edition)* **2003**
- *MasterFILE: updated database from EBSCO Publishing* **1993**
- *PASCAL, c/o Institute de L'Information Scientifique
  et Technique. Cross-disciplinary electronic database covering
  the fields of science, technology & medicine. Also available
  on CD-ROM, and can generate customized retrospective
  searches <http://www.inist.fr>* **1992**
- *Referativnyi Zhurnal (Abstracts Journal of the All-Russian
  Institute of Scientific and Technical Information-in Russian)* . . . **1986**
- *RESEARCH ALERT/ISI Alerting Services <http://www.isinet.com>* **2000**
- *ScienceDirect Navigator (Elsevier)
  <http://www.info.sciencedirect.com>* **2002**
- *Scopus (Elsevier) <http://www.info.scopus.com>* **2002**
- *SwetsWise <http://www.swets.com>* **2001**
- *Worldwide Political Science Abstracts (formerly: Political Science &
  Government Abstracts) <http://www.csa.com>* **1996**

*Exact start date to come.

*Special Bibliographic Notes related to special journal issues
(separates) and indexing/abstracting:*

- indexing/abstracting services in this list will also cover material in any "separate" that is co-published simultaneously with Haworth's special thematic journal issue or DocuSerial. Indexing/abstracting usually covers material at the article/chapter level.
- monographic co-editions are intended for either non-subscribers or libraries which intend to purchase a second copy for their circulating collections.
- monographic co-editions are reported to all jobbers/wholesalers/approval plans. The source journal is listed as the "series" to assist the prevention of duplicate purchasing in the same manner utilized for books-in-series.
- to facilitate user/access services all indexing/abstracting services are encouraged to utilize the co-indexing entry note indicated at the bottom of the first page of each article/chapter/contribution.
- this is intended to assist a library user of any reference tool (whether print, electronic, online, or CD-ROM) to locate the monographic version if the library has purchased this version but not a subscription to the source journal.
- individual articles/chapters in any Haworth publication are also available through the Haworth Document Delivery Service (HDDS).

ABOUT THE EDITOR

Gary Ives is Assistant Director of Acquisitions and Coordinator of Electronic Resources at Texas A&M University Libraries, College Station, TX. Earlier, he served as the Associate Director for Information Resources at the Medical Sciences Library, Texas A&M University. In those positions, he has managed licensing of and access to electronic resources. Gary has also managed document delivery services at the Medical Sciences Library, Texas A&M University; the Moody Medical Library, University of Texas Medical Branch at Galveston; the University Library, University of Texas at El Paso; and the Claude Moore Health Sciences Library, University of Virginia. He has served on various resource sharing and collection development committees for TexShare (Texas Resource Sharing), the South Central Chapter of the Medical Library Association, the Greater Western Library Alliance, and the American Library Association. Gary currently serves as a member of the ALA SHARES Licensing and Legislation Committee; a member of the ALA SHARES Interlibrary Loan Committee; chair of the ALA ALCTS SS Journal Costs Discussion Group; and co-chair of the Collection Development Committee of the Greater Western Library Alliance. He holds memberships in ALA, TLA, and NASIG. His degrees are from Bethany College, WV (BA), and from the University of Pittsburgh (MLS).

To Larry Frye with life-long gratitude for recommending the Profession to me, and me to the Profession.

Electronic Journal Management Systems: Experiences from the Field

CONTENTS

Introduction   1
    Gary Ives

The Master Serial List at Montana State University–
    A Simple, Easy to Use Approach   3
    Susan P. Marshall
    Jodee L. Kawasaki

Electronic Resource Management: Transition from In-House
    to In-House/Vendor Approach   17
    Robert Alan

One-Stop: Serials Management with TDNet   27
    Peggy S. Cooper
    Dan Lester

Taming the E-Journal Jungle: The University of South Carolina's
    Experience with TDNet   35
    Karen McMullen
    Derek Wilmott

Implementing EBSCO's A-to-Z and LinkSource Products
    for Improved Electronic Journal Management   43
    Virginia A. Lingle

Evolutionary Approach to Managing E-Resources   55
    Richard P. Jasper
    Laura Sheble

Transition to E-Journals at Texas A&M University, 1995-2004   71
  Gary Ives

Can SFX Replace Your Homegrown Periodicals Holding List?
  How the University of Wisconsin-La Crosse
  Made the Transition   79
  Jenifer S. Holman

Customized Electronic Resources Management System
  for a Multi-Library University: Viewpoint from One Library 89
  Janis F. Brown
  Janet L. Nelson
  Maggie Wineburgh-Freed

Integrating and Streamlining Electronic Resources Workflows
  via Innovative's Electronic Resource Management   103
  Laura Tull
  Janet Crum
  Trisha Davis
  C. Rockelle Strader

Electronic Resources Management Systems: The Experience
  of Beta Testing and Implementation   125
  Tony A. Harvell

Beginning to See the Light: Developing a Discourse
  for Electronic Resource Management   137
  Jill Emery

Index   149

Introduction

Do you remember when libraries had no photocopiers?
Those younger than 45 don't.

Do you remember when libraries had no computers?
Those younger than 30 don't.

Do you remember when libraries had no electronic journals?
Our current students don't!

Each of the papers in this collection is a testimonial to the "explosive growth," the "burgeoning popularity," and the "daunting challenges of managing" electronic journals in libraries. Susan Marshall and Jodee Kawasaki (Montana State University), and Robert Alan (Pennsylvania State University) describe management tools developed locally. Peggy Cooper and Dan Lester (Boise State University), and Karen McMullen and Derek Wilmott (University of South Carolina) describe their libraries' experiences with TDNet. Virginia Lingle (Pennsylvania State University, Hershey) describes the selection and implementation process at her library for EBSCO's A-to-Z and LinkSource products. Richard Jasper and Laura Sheble (Wayne State University), Gary Ives (Texas A&M University), Jenifer Holman (University of Wisconsin–La Crosse), and Janis Brown, Janet Nelson, and Maggie Wineburgh-Freed (University of Southern California, Norris Medical Library) discuss their institutions' evolution to SFX and other supporting systems. Laura Tull, Trisha Davis, and C. Rockelle Strader (Ohio State University), with Janet Crum (Oregon Health & Science University), and Tony Harvell (University of California San Diego) discuss their partnerships with Innovative Interfaces, Inc. in developing and beta testing an Electronic Resources Management System, built in conformity with emerging standards, and designed for interoperability with

[Haworth co-indexing entry note]: "Introduction." Ives, Gary. Co-published simultaneously in *The Serials Librarian* (The Haworth Information Press, an imprint of The Haworth Press, Inc.) Vol. 47, No. 4, 2005, pp. 1-2; and: *Electronic Journal Management Systems: Experiences from the Field* (ed: Gary Ives) The Haworth Information Press, an imprint of The Haworth Press, Inc., 2005, pp. 1-2. Single or multiple copies of this article are available for a fee from The Haworth Document Delivery Service [1-800-HAWORTH, 9:00 a.m. - 5:00 p.m. (EST). E-mail address: docdelivery@haworthpress.com].

http://www.haworthpress.com/web/SER
Digital Object Identifier: 10.1300/J123v47n04_01

existing systems. And, as a capstone, Jill Emery (University of Houston) presents an argument that, not just systems, but a new "discourse of electronic resource management," needs to be created to effectively manage and deliver these new information resources.

These papers were submitted in response to a call for papers I posted to the discussion lists in May 2004. I will be eternally grateful to these authors for answering the call. This project began with a chance phone call to the editor, Jim Cole, over a year ago. It would not have happened, nor would it have taken this form, without his enthusiasm, guidance, support, and patience at every stage, for which I don't know how to thank him enough. Personal thanks go to Jeanne Harrell, my supervisor, and to Stephen Atkins, my supervisor's supervisor, who both give good advice, active support, and warm encouragement every day of the year.

Gary Ives

The Master Serial List
at Montana State University–
A Simple, Easy to Use Approach

Susan P. Marshall
Jodee L. Kawasaki

SUMMARY. Two years ago, subscription information for serials in all formats at Montana State University (MSU) was located in various paper files, stored on a variety of PCs, or nonexistent. One system was desperately needed to track all subscriptions. Subscription management systems and the acquisitions modules of Integrated Library Systems were lacking and not flexible enough to include many of the new bundling and pricing models of serials. Librarians at MSU assembled a simple and easy to use serials tracking method for back-end management. This article describes how MSU uses Microsoft Excel to manage all of their serial subscriptions. *[Article copies available for a fee from The Haworth Document Delivery Service: 1-800-HAWORTH. E-mail address: <docdelivery@haworthpress. com> Website: <http://www.HaworthPress.com> © 2005 by The Haworth Press, Inc. All rights reserved.]*

Susan P. Marshall is Electronic Resources Librarian at Montana State University, Renne Library, P.O. Box 173320, Bozeman, MT 59717-3320 (E-mail: smarshall@montana.edu).

Jodee L. Kawasaki is Information Resources Development Team Leader at Montana State University, Renne Library, P.O. Box 173320, Bozeman, MT 59717-3320 (E-mail: alijk@montana.edu).

[Haworth co-indexing entry note]: "The Master Serial List at Montana State University–A Simple, Easy to Use Approach." Marshall, Susan P., and Jodee L. Kawasaki. Co-published simultaneously in *The Serials Librarian* (The Haworth Information Press, an imprint of The Haworth Press, Inc.) Vol. 47, No. 4, 2005, pp. 3-15; and: *Electronic Journal Management Systems: Experiences from the Field* (ed: Gary Ives) The Haworth Information Press, an imprint of The Haworth Press, Inc., 2005, pp. 3-15. Single or multiple copies of this article are available for a fee from The Haworth Document Delivery Service [1-800-HAWORTH, 9:00 a.m. - 5:00 p.m. (EST). E-mail address: docdelivery@haworthpress.com].

KEYWORDS. Electronic resources management, ERM, e-journal packages, serials management

INTRODUCTION

It is no surprise that in the last five years the management of serials has become a challenging and somewhat daunting task. This is largely due to both the demand for and increase in the number of available online resources. For many years, the print version was the only option available for any given serial title. Print subscriptions were purchased individually and processed by a subscription agent for the library. To keep the library informed of the status of their subscriptions and to make claims, librarians utilized a relatively straightforward management system provided by the subscription agent. Costs, publisher information and other subscription elements were recorded in the acquisitions modules of the library's Integrated Library Systems (ILS). This worked for individual subscriptions and still does, and at the same time the management of print and microform serials in the ILS remains problematic at times. Perfection with titles, ISSNs, frequency, etc., is nearly impossible. However, difficulty in the management of subscriptions really increased with the introduction of the electronic version. Even before the Internet, online access was available as publishers supplied floppies and CDs of single issues and the world of electronic access began. Thus another layer of complexity was added to serials acquisition and management through the introduction of the electronic format.

Today's users demand electronic access to library resources and they want it delivered right to their fingertips (desktop, laptop, etc.). In addition, this demand continues to increase at an accelerating rate. The scope of this user demand really hit home when a physics post doc student recently told a librarian at Montana State University that the value of the print version of his favorite journal title was nostalgia. As libraries respond to this demand, the acquisition and management of online subscriptions becomes increasingly complicated due to more choices such as the combination online + print or only online pricing, consortia pricing models, various title package configurations, and linking options to the full text to name a few. In addition, librarians at Montana State University in recent years have often found themselves dealing directly with their publishing partners in order to negotiate lower package pricing while leaving out the subscription agent. This alternative approach affords a benefit to the library in the form of a discount when paying directly to the publishing partner but it also then becomes the library's responsibility to maintain the title lists for each journal package. The downside of this, of course, is that it costs more of the librarian's time.

These are just some of the nuances of online resources that create record-keeping opportunities for those working with serials. Current subscription management systems and the acquisitions modules of Integrated Library Systems have been found to be lacking and do not have the flexibility to include many of these particulars.

In the fall of 2002, the Information Resources Development Team at Montana State University, led by Jodee Kawasaki, assembled a simple serial title tracking method for back-end management. Thus, the method is not designed for public nor cross-team access. This article describes that method in detail, but first, a little background.

THE SITUATION

Librarians at Montana State University have aggressively been transitioning their serial titles from print to online as fiscally as possible since 1999. They currently subscribe to 2900 print only titles and over 13,000 electronic journal titles (these include both journal packages and those titles within aggregators). Due to these relatively high numbers, the rapid rate of conversion from print to online, varying purchasing options, and a change in personnel in 2002, it soon became very difficult to track cost and bundling details for each of their titles. Also, institutional site licenses were not filed appropriately or not at all, so it was not clear with whom the negotiations were made and what the terms of the agreements were with some of their publishing partners.

For instance, with renewal season starting in August of 2002, several small bundles of titles with online access that had been purchased at a prior time were discovered, but no record of them was kept anywhere. Within the first year seven such packages were identified. This oversight occurred because subscription information about individual titles was located in various paper files, stored on a variety of PCs or nonexistent. There were titles in the subscription agent's renewal list for print, titles on the UMI invoices for microform, and titles on paper lists for most of the e-journal packages to which MSU subscribed. As part of the daily operation of the Information Resources Department, information about serial titles was needed. Oftentimes, the MSU Information Resources team members found themselves routinely spending a lot of time digging for information about a serial other than the paper holdings, which were listed in the online catalog. The information required was as simple as: from whom did MSU purchase that title or how much does that title cost and is it cheaper in a different format?

Needless to say, the accurate record keeping of the arrangements held with each publishing partner is critical for the purposes of financial management and auditing. Up until that time, a centralized tracking system did not exist that was flexible enough to handle all of the peculiarities of serials management and comprehensive enough to include serials titles in all formats. A centralized program that contained complete subscription information, especially pricing and bundling data and that could identify redundancy in online and print title purchases, was desperately needed. Also, the system had to be designed quickly and be simple to use so that anyone could step in at any skill level and alter its data with ease.

THE SOLUTION

A sophisticated program that utilizes MYSQL to create a relational database could have been developed locally, or a commercial relational database could have been purchased and adjusted to the environment at Montana State University. The resources for the development of a comprehensive database of the magnitude required were not available at the time within the library. The commercially available relational database was not an option either due to the set up and training necessary. The decision was made to wait for a commercially available electronic resources management system for serials and in the interim, to set up a Microsoft Excel spreadsheet to keep track of all of their serial titles in one place.

The advantages of using Excel are that it is simple to use, requires very little training or library knowledge, and its data can be exported into other commercially available products. Thus, institutions of any size can set up their data elements into columns and start entering their information within minutes. Later on, data elements can be added without calling in a programmer or someone familiar with the product in order to adjust relational tables as in the locally designed database model. Accordingly, there doesn't need to be a resident expert/designer available at all times to assist in problem solving. The motivational design of this system was its simplicity and ease of use and as a result, in the fall of 2002, the Master Serial List was born.

THE DESIGN AND LAYOUT

In the initial set up phase of the spreadsheet, specific data elements were chosen. Librarians had to ask the following questions to determine which of those elements to include and how to express them:

What does MSU own? [Title]
How much did MSU pay for it? [03, 04, 05]
From which account does the money come? [Subscription Agent or Local]
Who is the publishing partner? [Journal packages]
How is the title bundled? [Package or Individually]
Is it print, microform, print + online, or online only?

The very first spreadsheet had four data elements in six columns: Title, Price, Vendor, and Format. (The Format element had 3 columns, one each for

Print, Electronic, and Microform.) As time went on, more data elements were added for reference, standing order, special collections and locations of extended campuses' Nursing titles.

At the present, there are 8,241 titles (rows) and 18 data elements (columns) in MSU's Master Serials List: Title, ISSN (electronic and print), Price (02, 03, 04, 05), LC Class, Paid By (EBSCO or Direct), Package Name, Print (Yes or No), Electronic (Y/N), Notes, Reference (Y/N), Newspaper (Y/N), Dbase (Y/N), Standing Order (Y/N), Microform (Y/N), Other campuses (Billings, Missoula, Bozeman, Great Falls), Membership (Y/N), Nursing (Y/N), Canceled (Y/N).

This is admittedly a large spreadsheet and a bit cumbersome in design for accessing information, but it is straightforward and supplies the information that is needed. The Yes/No format is used to add flexibility to export data into a relational database in the future, if desired. Also, Excel sorts and filters without much effort, giving out the targeted serials information quickly. Columns can be "hidden" so that specific data elements can be viewed on the screen side-by-side.

A second spreadsheet, called the "Journal Package Pricing Report," was designed to provide more information at the journal package level for more specific vendor pricing and contact details. In the future, licensing information will be included in this second spreadsheet. Figures 5 and 6 toward the end of this article show two of its screenshots with a brief explanation immediately following.

The first column on the Master Serial List (see Figure 1) is the "Title." This can be the title of the serial or the name of the journal package or database. An asterisk is used to indicate journal packages and databases in order to keep these items at the top of the list when sorting within the spreadsheet. The price at the journal package or database level represents the price for all of the titles within that package or the price of the database.

Take note that individual title names are repeated for each format. For example, in Figure 1, Rows 14 and 15 both show "Academy of management journal." Row 14 represents the print version of this title. Under the "Print" column, Column J, a "Yes" is indicated and the "Electronic" column, Column K, has been left blank. Along these same lines, Row 15 represents the electronic version of this title and will indicate a "Yes" under the "Electronic" column, Column K, and the "Print" column has been left blank. This also holds true for the repeated title: "Academy of management review" in Rows 16 and 17.

Also, notice that rows 15 and 17 do not show a Price figure. These rows represent the electronic format and are part of the Jstor B package (see Column I). There should not be a price on a title that has a package name in its Column I. In these cases, there will be a price on the journal package title itself (Column A) and this name will have an asterisk preceding it (e.g., *Jstor B Package). This is done so that the user can sort the spreadsheet by Column I, "Package," to discover exactly which titles are part of each package. Therefore, package

FIGURE 1. Master Serial List–First Six Data Elements

Title	E-ISS	Print ISSN	Price '02	Price'03	Price '04	LC	Paid By	Package	Print	Electron
°Acoustical society of America			1270	1335	1435		Ebsco	AIP		Yes
°American anthropological association package			515	447	447	GN	Ebsco	American anthro assoc	Yes	
°American association of physics teachers					824		Ebsco	AIP		Yes
°American physiological society					5970		Ebsco	APS		Yes
°Geological society of America					1350		Ebsco	GSA		Yes
°Science					4375		Direct	AAS		Yes
365/AIGA				77.58	76.5	NC	Ebsco		Yes	
A + U, architecture and urbanism		0389-9160	346	386	317	NA	Ebsco		Yes	
Abstracts in social gerontology		1047-4862	395	435	542	HQ	Ebsco		Yes	
Abstracts of American society of animal science		0198-9863		0	0	SF	Ebsco	J of animal science	Yes	
Academy of accounting historians membership			55	55	55	HF	Ebsco	Acad of acc hist memb	Yes	
Academy of management executive		1079-5545	110	110	110	HD	Ebsco		Yes	
Academy of management journal		0001-4273	125	140	140	HD	Ebsco		Yes	
Academy of management journal		0001-4273	0	0	0	HD	Direct	Jstor B		Yes
Academy of management review		0363-7425	105	140	140	HD	Ebsco		Yes	
Academy of management review		0363-7425	0	0	0	HD	Direct	Jstor B		Yes
Accounting historians journal		0148-4184	0	0	0	HF	Ebsco	Acad of acc hist memb	Yes	
Accounting historians notebook		1075-1416			0	HF	Ebsco	Acad of acc hist memb	Yes	
Accounting horizons		0888-7993		0	0	HF	Ebsco	Accounting review combo	Yes	
Accounting perspectives				30		HF	Ebsco		Yes	
Accounting review		0001-4826	350	355	450	HF	Ebsco	Accounting review combo	Yes	
Accounting review		0001-4826	0	0	0	HF	Direct	Jstor B		Yes

names are consistent for all of its titles. For example, if a "Package" name for one title is "Jstor B" it cannot be "Jstor B" for a different title in the same package. This is critical for sorting and filtering because there is no provision within Excel to recognize that these terms mean one in the same.

Incidentally, Row 21, "Accounting perspectives," does not have a "Price" nor a "Package," which means the title was canceled. A note will appear in the Note field (Column P) to confirm this and a "Yes" appears in the "Canceled" column.

Row 12, "Academy of accounting historians membership," shows a price of $55. The "Package" column, Column I, will reveal the titles on this screenshot that are a part of that membership, Rows 18 and 19. The titles on these two rows do not have a price because they come with the Academy's membership. This is an illustration of a Print package or combination.

"Accounting review," Row 22, is another example of a print combination. "Accounting review" indicates its package price in Column F and Column I shows the title, "Accounting horizons," Row 20, as part of the "Accounting review" combination. Also note that "Accounting review" comes in electronic format, indicated by Row 23 and is part of the Jstor B package.

Column G represents the LC classification. This column can be used to sort and view the collection as a whole by LC class for the purposes of collection development and accreditation.

An example of flexibility with the Excel spreadsheet method is the later addition of ISSNs both print and electronic (where available). The scope of a recent ISSN project was to add the print ISSNs first with the electronic ISSNs to be inserted later.

The "Paid By," Column H, in Figure 2 specifies who is paying the publishing partner. "Ebsco" means the subscription is paid out of the library's Ebsco account, "Direct" indicates the money will come from the local library account, "Proquest" means Proquest pays for the subscription out of the library's Proquest account, "Gift" signifies a gift to the library.

In Figure 2 the title "American demographics" is listed twice, once for print and again for the microform format, both indicating a price. Under the column "Microform" (not part of this screenshot), Column V, there is a "Yes."

Rows 11 and 12 for the title "American ethnologist" do not show a price in either row. This is because the title is part of a print as well as an electronic package. Row 11, Column H indicates the name of the print package and like-

FIGURE 2. Second Example of the Master Serial List

Title	E-IS	Print ISSN	Price '02	Price'03	Price '04	LC	Paid By	Package	Print	Electron
American craft		0194-8008	50	50	50	NK	Ebsco		Yes	
American demographics		0163-4089	69	58	58	HB	Ebsco		Yes	
American demographics		0163-4089	63		75.4	HB	Proquest			
American economic association quarterly		1532-5059			0		Direct	Jstor A&S I+B		Yes
American economic review		0002-8282	140	205	250	HB	Ebsco	American economic review	Yes	
American economic review		0002-8282	0	0	0	HB	Direct	Jstor A&S I+B		Yes
American educational research journal		0002-8312	77	120	120	L	Ebsco		Yes	
American educator		0148-432X	0		0	L	Gift		Yes	
American entomologist		1046-2821	77	80	82	QL	Ebsco		Yes	
American ethnologist		0094-0496	0	0	0	GN	Ebsco	American anthro assoc	Yes	
American ethnologist		0094-0496	0	0	0	GN	Direct	Jstor A&S II		Yes
American family physician		0002-838X			0	R	Direct			Yes
American family physician		0002-838X	115	144	0	R	Ebsco		Yes	
American fern journal		0002-8444			0		Direct	Bioone		Yes
American gardener		1087-9978		0	0	SB	Ebsco	Amer horticultural society	Yes	
American heart journal		0002-8703	371	190	179	RC	Ebsco		Yes	
American heritage		0002-8738	32	24	24	E	Ebsco		Yes	
American historical review		0002-8762	0	0	0	E	Direct	Jstor A&S I		Yes
American historical review		0002-8762	120	250	250	E	Ebsco		Yes	
American horticultural society membership			55	55	55	SB	Ebsco	Amer horticultural society	Yes	
American illustration		0737-6642	71	65	65	NC	Ebsco		Yes	
American imago		0065-860X	0		0	BF	Direct	Muse Project		Yes
American imago		0065-860X	107	112		BF	Ebsco		Yes	

wise Row 12 Column H shows the name of the electronic package. (Both formats are active since Jstor has a 5-year embargo for their electronic access, it follows then that the print must remain active for the most recent 5 years.)

The title "American family physician" is also listed twice: Row 13 for the electronic format and Row 14 for the print. Neither formats are showing a Price for '04. Upon examination of the "Notes" column of Row 13, the electronic is now free online, and for Row 14, the "Canceled" column indicates a "Yes."

Neither Rows 23 and 24 for the title "American imago" have a price. Row 23 shows the "Package" as MUSE Project. This means that this title is part of the MUSE Project online package and the total price will appear under the "Title," Column A, as "*MUSE Project." Row 24 does not show a price for the print format because according to the Note column, the print was canceled to avoid redundancy with the electronic subscription. Figures 3 and 4 illustrate just two of the pricing and packaging nuances connected with online resources.

The Master Serial List in Figure 3 was filtered by "Springer" in Column I, "Package." The site license agreement with Springer requires that the library maintain its subscription to 41 original print titles in order to qualify for the en-

FIGURE 3. Package Pricing Model–Springer Titles

Microsoft Excel - Figure 3

	A	B	C	F	I	J	K	L
1								
2	Title	E-ISSN	Print ISSN	Price '04	Package	Print	Electronic	Notes
3	Polymer bulletin	1436-244	0170-0839	0	Springer		Yes	
4	Population ecology		1438-3896	313	Springer	Yes		Must keep print title for Springer package.
5	Population ecology		1438-3896	0	Springer		Yes	
6	Primates		0032-8332	0	Springer		Yes	
7	Probability theory and related fields	1432-206	0178-8051	0	Springer		Yes	
8	Progress in colloid and polymer science		0340-255X	0	Springer		Yes	
9	Protoplasma		0033-183X	0	Springer		Yes	
10	Psychological research		0340-0727	0	Springer		Yes	
11	Psychological research		0340-0727	880	Springer	Yes		Must keep print title for Springer package.
12	Psychopharmacology		0033-3158	0	Springer		Yes	
13	Psychotherapeut	1432-208	0935-6185	0	Springer		Yes	
14	Publications mathematiques de l'IHES	1618-191	0073-8301	0	Springer		Yes	
15	Pure and applied geophysics	1420-913	0033-4553	0	Springer		Yes	
16	Radiation and environmental biophysics	1432-209	0301-634X	0	Springer		Yes	
17	Radiologe	1432-210	0033-832X	0	Springer		Yes	
18	Rechtsmedizin	1434-519	0937-9819	0	Springer		Yes	
19	Regional environmental change	1436-378	1436-3798	0	Springer		Yes	
20	Reproduktionsmedizin	1434-808	1434-6931	0	Springer		Yes	
21	Requirements engineering	1432-010	0947-3602	0	Springer		Yes	
22	Research and theory for nursing practice		1541-6577	134	Springer	Yes		Must keep print title for Springer package. Print only.
23	Research in engineering design	1435-606	0934-9839	0	Springer		Yes	
24	Research in experimental medicine		0300-9130	0	Springer		Yes	

Sheet1 / Sheet2 / Sheet3

Ready

FIGURE 4. Consortia Pricing Model–Wiley Interscience

Microsoft Excel - Figure 4

A1 = Title

	A	B	C	F	G	I	J	K	L
1	Title	E-ISSN	Print ISSN	Price '04	LC	Package	Print	Electronic	Notes
2	Geological journal		0072-1050	0		Wiley		Yes	
3	Head and neck		1043-3074	0	RD	Wiley		Yes	
4	Heat transfer - Asian research	1523-149	1099-2871	0		Wiley		Yes	
5	Helvetica chimica acta		0018-019X	0	QD	Wiley		Yes	
6	Heteroatom chemistry		1042-7163	0	QD	Wiley		Yes	
7	Human resource management		0090-4848	0	HF	Wiley		Yes	Price based on 1 of original 48 print titles. List price plus 10%.
8	Hydrological processes	1099-108	0885-6087	0	GB	Wiley		Yes	
9	Infant and child development	1522-721	1522-7227	0	HQ	Wiley		Yes	
10	International journal for numerical and analytical methods in geomechanics		0363-9061	0	TA	Wiley		Yes	
11	International journal for numerical methods in engineering		0029-5981	0	TA	Wiley		Yes	Price based on 1 of original 48 print titles. List price plus 10%.
12	International journal for numerical methods in fluids		0271-2091	0	QA3	Wiley		Yes	
13	International journal of adaptive control and signal processing		0890-6327	0	TJ	Wiley		Yes	Price based on 1 of original 48 print titles. List price plus 10%.
14	International journal of cancer		0020-7136	0		Wiley		Yes	
15	International journal of chemical kinetics		0538-8066	0	QD	Wiley		Yes	
16	International journal of climatology		0899-8418	0	QC	Wiley		Yes	
17	International journal of energy research	1099-114	0363-907X	0	TJ	Wiley		Yes	
18	International journal of imaging systems and technology	1098-109	0899-9457	0	TK	Wiley		Yes	
19	International journal of intelligent systems	1098-111	0884-8173	0	Q	Wiley		Yes	
20	International journal of network management		1055-7148	0	TK	Wiley		Yes	
	International journal of quantum								

Sheet1 / Sheet2 / Sheet3 /

Ready

tire package of online titles offered by Springer. While all Springer package titles are listed in the Master Serial List, these 41 specific titles are set apart from the rest on the spreadsheet through the use of the "Notes" column. The "Notes" column will have the designation, "Must keep print title for Springer package" on each of the 41 original titles. In Figure 3, three of the titles have "Notes" fields. Two of these titles, "Population ecology" and "Psychological research," are repeated in the "Title" column, which indicates that they come in both print and electronic formats. The third title "Research and theory for nursing practice" has a "Note" that indicates this title comes in print only with no electronic counterpart (yet). The total price for the Springer package can be found under Column A, "Title," and is listed as "*Springer Package."

Also, as the reader may have noted by now, the spreadsheet is flexible enough that it doesn't matter in what order the formats are listed for any given title. Sometimes the print format of a title is listed first and at other times, the electronic format is listed first.

The Master Serial List in Figure 4 was filtered by "Wiley" in Column I, "Package." The Wiley Interscience site license and pricing for Montana State University is consortia based. Libraries in the AISTI (Alliance for Innovation in Science and Technology Information) consortium have access to Wiley titles in each other's collections. The price each library pays is based on the current print price of their original titles prior to the Wiley deal, plus 10%. The library does not continue to order and receive the print but their price is based on the current price of those original titles. Montana State University subscribed to 48 print titles before participating in the AISTI program. Figure 4 shows three of those original titles designated by the "Notes" column. The "Electronic" column denotes "Yes" for all of the titles. There are no print copies sent to the library. Since the cost is not exactly the price of the print, there are no prices indicated for the original print titles. This list serves as a reminder of the original print titles for future pricing purposes. The price of the Wiley package can be found at the title: "*Wiley e-journal access" in Column A.

As mentioned earlier, a second spreadsheet, called the "Journal Package Pricing Report," was designed to provide information at the journal package level for more specific vendor pricing and contact details. Figure 5 shows some of the elements of the spreadsheet: "Number of titles," "Package price," "Web access price," "Consortia deal," "Format," "Paid by" and "Paid to." This sheet serves to not only keep track of what has been purchased and for how much, but also to indicate who made the deal, the format of the titles, who

FIGURE 5. Journal Package Pricing Report

Journal Packages / Databases	# of Titles	2004 Price	2004 Charge for Web Access	Consortium Deal Through	Format	Paid by	Paid to:
Annual Reviews	29	XXXXXX		AISTI	Online only	Ebsco	AISTI
BioOne + The Arabidopsis Book (A serial)	65	XXXXXX		AISTI	Online only	Ebsco	AISTI
Blackwell Synergy	336	XXXXXX	XXXXXX	AISTI	Print+Online	Print -Ebsco Access fee - Direct	Blackwell
Cambridge University Press ($4070 paid for 2003 access of all titles)	175	XXXXXX			Online only	Ebsco	Cambridge
CSIRO (Commonwealth Scientific...)	5	XXXXXX			Online only	Ebsco	CSIRO
Dekker	82	XXXXXX		ESIG	Online only	Ebsco	Dekker
Elsevier Journals (+ Academic Press) (1477+ 182)	1659	XXXXXX			Online only	MSU	Elsevier
Emerald Journals	135	XXXXXX		BCR	Online + 2 Print	Print - Ebsco Access fee - Direct	Emerald
Geological Society of America	3	XXXXXX			Print+Online	Ebsco	GSA
IEEE AASP Electronic package	117	XXXXXX			Online only	Ebsco	IEEE
IEEE Spectrum online	1	XXXXXX			Online only	Ebsco	IEEE
IOP (EBSCO pays AIP)	65	XXXXXX	XXXXXX	AISTI	Online + 5 Org. Print	AISTI for electronic access, Ebsco for print/online	AISTI for electronic access AIP for Print
JSTOR - Arts & Science I (117 total)	117	XXXXXX	XXXXXX	JSTOR	Online only	MSU	JSTOR

pays for the online access and who pays for the print copies as well as the publishing partner.

Journal package elements that are not visible on this screen but are listed in other columns are: specific MSU campuses that subscribe to each package and the number of simultaneous users allowed for each package.

Figure 6 shows more elements that are tracked on the "Journal Package Pricing Report": "Subscription length," "Notes," "Contact" person, their "E-mail" address, and "Phone" number. These are very important elements not only to have available when problems arise with the subscription, but also for preparing for future contract negotiation. License agreement specifics will be tracked on this sheet in the future.

CONCLUSION

The purpose of the original design of the Master Serial List at Montana State University was to provide one place where all data about serial subscriptions could be stored. The Microsoft Excel spreadsheet method was a quick

FIGURE 6. Journal Package Pricing Report–Scrolled Over

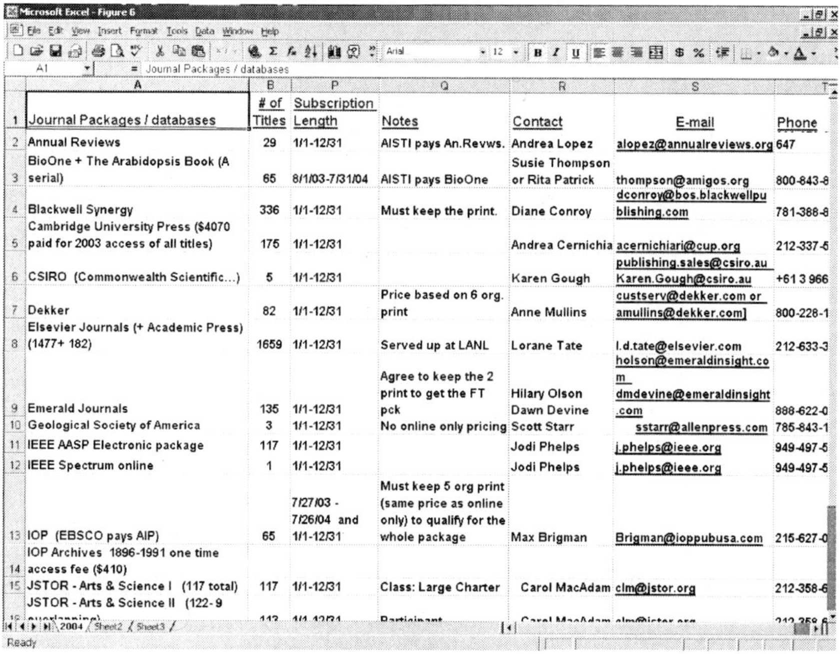

	A	B	P	Q	R	S	T
1	Journal Packages / databases	# of Titles	Subscription Length	Notes	Contact	E-mail	Phone
2	Annual Reviews	29	1/1-12/31	AISTI pays An.Revws.	Andrea Lopez	alopez@annualreviews.org	647
3	BioOne + The Arabidopsis Book (A serial)	65	8/1/03-7/31/04	AISTI pays BioOne	Susie Thompson or Rita Patrick	thompson@amigos.org	800-843-8
4	Blackwell Synergy	336	1/1-12/31	Must keep the print.	Diane Conroy	dconroy@bos.blackwellpublishing.com	781-388-8
5	Cambridge University Press ($4070 paid for 2003 access of all titles)	175	1/1-12/31		Andrea Cernichia	acernichiari@cup.org	212-337-5
6	CSIRO (Commonwealth Scientific...)	5	1/1-12/31		Karen Gough	publishing.sales@csiro.au Karen.Gough@csiro.au	+61 3 966
7	Dekker	82	1/1-12/31	Price based on 6 org. print	Anne Mullins	custserv@dekker.com or amullins@dekker.com]	800-228-1
8	Elsevier Journals (+ Academic Press) (1477+ 182)	1659	1/1-12/31	Served up at LANL	Lorane Tate	l.d.tate@elsevier.com	212-633-3
9	Emerald Journals	135	1/1-12/31	Agree to keep the 2 print to get the FT pck	Hilary Olson Dawn Devine	holson@emeraldinsight.com dmdevine@emeraldinsight.com	888-622-0
10	Geological Society of America	3	1/1-12/31	No online only pricing	Scott Starr	sstarr@allenpress.com	785-843-1
11	IEEE AASP Electronic package	117	1/1-12/31		Jodi Phelps	j.phelps@ieee.org	949-497-5
12	IEEE Spectrum online	1	1/1-12/31		Jodi Phelps	j.phelps@ieee.org	949-497-5
13	IOP (EBSCO pays AIP)	65	7/27/03 - 7/26/04 and 1/1-12/31	Must keep 5 org print (same price as online only) to qualify for the whole package	Max Brigman	Brigman@ioppubusa.com	215-627-0
14	IOP Archives 1896-1991 one time access fee ($410)						
15	JSTOR - Arts & Science I (117 total)	117	1/1-12/31	Class: Large Charter	Carol MacAdam	clm@jstor.org	212-358-6
16	JSTOR - Arts & Science II (122-9 overlapping)	113	1/1-12/31	Participant	Carol MacAdam	clm@jstor.org	212-358-6

way to get up and running in a short amount of time. While data entry was very time consuming and required a high level of detail, it was a small price to pay for the ease of use in finding specific information formerly located in several places within the Information Resources Department.

The Master Serial List has been in use for two full years. It has been enlarged continuously based on need–information needed. There are now 8,241 titles tracked with 18 data elements each. The spreadsheet form of the Master Serial List works well for Montana State University. The "Hide" feature of Excel allows a condensed view of the spreadsheet. By using its "Filter" function, accreditation and other reports can be run. When sorting the Master Serial List, total dollars paid to a publishing partner are figured or cancellations are counted. The burden of scattered record keeping found two years ago is gone. The almost effortless functionality allows the Information Resources team members to quickly discover answers to inquiries of any serial. They can access it, manipulate it and run a quick report. During the past six months, a temporary hire employee added data and new columns, and a student worker most recently added the latest renewal list/invoice information. The ease of using the spreadsheet is vital. The simplicity of entering data into the spreadsheet and how the data elements are expressed is paramount to the success of the acquisition and management of serials. Thus the Master Serial List is large, yet very functional. Keeping it simple still works for Montana State University.

While its simplicity is its best feature, it is not without its limitations. As mentioned earlier, there is no Web-enabled public or cross-team access to the spreadsheet. However, this has not affected its usability in the least bit. The purpose of the List in its design was for access only by the Information Resources Department personnel through a shared network drive in order to manage where the money was going and how much was left toward the end of the fiscal year. As a result, the creation of the Master Serial List revealed a $100,000 savings in our total subscription costs for 2003 and thus has proven itself to be a reliable source for yearly budget analysis and reporting.

A downside to its simplicity is that it is somewhat "clunky" in accessing information because it uses sorting and filtering rather than a search feature. Its "Find" feature is not always precise enough or at times too precise. Along these same lines, there is lack of flexibility in reporting since it is not a relational database and comparisons are not run very easily. However, at this time the team at Montana State University is satisfied with the simple sort and filter features in order to extract the information they require.

This article contains just some of the factors that were considered when it came time to decide whether to build an advanced system locally or use a packaged software and adjust it to the environment at Montana State University. The jury is still out on whether to design that advanced system locally or not. As commercial electronic resource management systems appear on the market, they will be evaluated on all of the factors discussed in this article.

The extent of the irregularities in the ever-changing world of serials management run the spectrum from publisher bundling and library/consortium specific pricing to license agreement particulars. The question to ask then, of the new commercial products as they arise is not "Can the system right out of the box track data in the way the library needs it tracked?," but rather "Does the system have the flexibility built into it so that it can be adjusted to meet the tracking needs of each library?"

Until this type of system is available commercially, MSU will continue to use its simple approach in the successful management of their serial collection.

Electronic Resource Management: Transition from In-House to In-House/Vendor Approach

Robert Alan

SUMMARY. Keeping track of electronic resources is challenging. Libraries have adopted a variety of in-house approaches to keep track of electronic resources. Penn State Libraries' ERLIC (Electronic Resource Licensing Center) database is one such example of an in-house electronic resource management system. ERLIC (a Microsoft Access database) was originally designed to improve management of electronic resource licensing data and to generate Penn State's A-Z list. However, library vendors are now answering the call for solutions that may better integrate the management of electronic resources within the framework of evolving standards and library management system development. *[Article copies available for a fee from The Haworth Document Delivery Service: 1-800-HAWORTH. E-mail address: <docdelivery@ haworthpress.com> Website: <http://www.HaworthPress.com> © 2005 by The Haworth Press, Inc. All rights reserved.]*

KEYWORDS. Electronic resource management, electronic resources, electronic journals

Robert Alan, MLS, is Head of the Serials Department, The Pennsylvania State University, 126 Paterno Library, University Park, PA 16802 (E-mail: roal@psulias.psu.edu).

[Haworth co-indexing entry note]: "Electronic Resource Management: Transition from In-House to In-House/Vendor Approach." Alan, Robert. Co-published simultaneously in *The Serials Librarian* (The Haworth Information Press, an imprint of The Haworth Press, Inc.) Vol. 47, No. 4, 2005, pp. 17-25; and: *Electronic Journal Management Systems: Experiences from the Field* (ed: Gary Ives) The Haworth Information Press, an imprint of The Haworth Press, Inc., 2005, pp. 17-25. Single or multiple copies of this article are available for a fee from The Haworth Document Delivery Service [1-800-HAWORTH, 9:00 a.m. - 5:00 p.m. (EST). E-mail address: docdelivery@haworthpress.com].

INTRODUCTION

During the past ten years there has been exponential growth in the number of electronic journals, online citation databases, and online full-text aggregations acquired by libraries. Penn State Libraries is no exception, as the financial investment in electronic resources increases while funding for print resources declines. This shift in the collections budget will continue for the foreseeable future as print resources are cancelled due to budgetary constraints and the need to free up funds to support continuation of the large electronic journal and database packages, as well as acquisition of new resources. Library user expectations have risen, as faculty, staff, and students (especially those in science, technology, and medicine) are now demanding 24/7 access to resources formerly only available in the library or via document delivery.

Keeping track of electronic resources has provided libraries with many challenges and only partial solutions have been developed. Integrated library management systems do not support the unique complexities of electronic resource management. Locally developed solutions have included a combination of paper files, spreadsheets, and stand-alone databases. In-house electronic resource management systems were developed at a number of sites such as MIT (VERA-Virtual Electronic Access), Johns Hopkins (HERMES-*H*opkins *E*lectronic *R*esources *Manag*ement *S*ystem), UCLA (Digital Acquisitions Database), and The Tri-College Consortium (E-resources Tracking System [ERTS]).[1] The locally designed systems support some aspects of electronic resource management within their institutions. In-house development 'has helped identify and test functional data requirements, data streams, and workflows.

The landscape is now changing due to the development of standards. The Digital Library Federation (DLF) Electronic Resource Management Initiative (ERMI) addressed the functional data requirements, workflows, and data transfer based on input from both the library and vendor community.[2] Other agencies such as the NISO EDItEUR Joint Working Party on the Exchange of Serials Subscription Information (JWP) are addressing important issues related to electronic resource management. Standards will provide the necessary foundation for long-term advances in the way electronic resources are acquired and managed.

The second change has been vendor response to library market demand. Libraries are demanding products and services that support management and delivery of electronic content.

The following article will discuss Penn State's rationale for developing ERLIC (Electronic Licensing Information Center) and the future of the in-house database given the current developments in the library marketplace.

ERLIC DEVELOPMENT

In 1998 Penn State Libraries concluded that there was an immediate need to keep better track of electronic resources. Critical documentation, such as licenses, copies of invoices, and correspondence was maintained in paper format in technical services and a few other locations. The files were not secure and all too often information or the entire file might be missing or misfiled resulting in additional staff time needed to locate or reconstruct data. Critical documentation was also not accessible to many stakeholders outside of technical services.

In addition to critical documentation, there was also a need to better track electronic resources from initial request, through ordering, activation, and renewal. In 1998, Penn State's homegrown library management system (LIAS [Library Information Access System]) and commercial library management system vendors did not support the data elements, data streams, or workflows needed to effectively manage electronic resources. While orders were maintained in the acquisitions module of LIAS, there was no mechanism other than paper files and spreadsheets available to manage the licensing data.

An important part of the tracking process is insuring that stakeholders have access to information related to the status of orders, licensing restrictions, access issues, etc. In a large multi-campus environment such as Penn State, communication between stakeholders such as subject selectors, systems staff, and technical services staff is crucial. A decision was then made to begin planning development of an in-house database for electronic resource management. The growing number of electronic resources combined with user demand for electronic resources required immediate action.

A needs assessment of primary stakeholders from technical services, the business office, public services, collection development, and systems resulted in a list of information requirements. Stakeholders indicated a need to know:

- Status of a request for an electronic resource
- Funding and costs
- Status of payments and dates of renewals
- Product content and coverage
- Proposed and finalized license agreements
- Access limitations (e.g., number of simultaneous users)
- Usage data
- Title level access to electronic resources including full-text aggregations (A-Z list)

In response to stakeholders needs, ERLIC (a Microsoft Access database) was developed in 1998/1999.[3] ERLIC coverage included budgetary support, critical licensing information, order information, access information, usage data, and the facility to generate reports and statistics. ERLIC was designed to track orders, payments, and the status of renewals. Licensing data included access and authentication information, ILL restrictions, and e-reserves restrictions. A set of predefined reports was developed based on stakeholders needs, including generation of some ARL (Association for Research Libraries) statistics.

Critical licensing, access, authentication, and payment information was maintained at the resource record level for electronic journal packages (e.g., Elsevier ScienceDirect) and full-text aggregations (e.g., Proquest). Title level records were either created in ERLIC for the electronic journal packages or loaded when made available by information providers for full-text aggregations.

ERLIC was used to generate the A-Z electronic resource holdings list. Since ERLIC only contained content for paid resources, users also needed to rely on the online catalog for access to both paid and free electronic resources. However, until MARC record sets were made available, the online catalog did not contain title analytics for most full-text aggregations.

In 2001, Penn State migrated from its in-house library management system (LIAS) to the SIRSI Unicorn integrated library management system. This was a significant move away from a culture of in-house system development to one of partnering with commercial system and software vendors. (See Figure 1 for a graphic representation of the relationship between ERLIC, Cold ERLIC, and SIRSI Unicorn.)

COLD ERLIC

Unfortunately, once ERLIC was fully populated, access to the content rich database was too limited to meet all stakeholders' information needs. In response, Cold Fusion Web pages were developed in 2001 to enhance access to tracking, access, and authentication information. Data was extracted from ERLIC (Microsoft Access) and loaded into the Cold ERLIC database on a monthly basis. While improving access to some information, the workloads associated with extracting, loading, and indexing data were considerable.

ERLIC LIMITATIONS

As a Microsoft Access database, ERLIC quickly became very large and cumbersome to update and query. Staff time required to manage ERLIC increased significantly over a relatively brief period of time. Data extracts needed to update the Cold ERLIC Web pages took longer to process. In addition to staffing and workload considerations, the information needs of many stakeholders were not being met. The Cold ERLIC Web pages were helpful but incomplete. There continued to be a need to maintain multiple paper copies of license agreements, invoices, and correspondence in technical service files.

FIGURE 1. The relationship between ERLIC, Cold ERLIC, and SIRSI Unicorn.

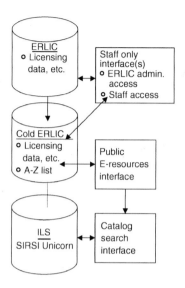

ERLIC²

In 2002/2003 a new Web version of ERLIC called ERLIC² was developed and released.[4] The goal of ERLIC² was to improve the overall management of electronic resources and access to those resources. ERLIC² was designed to provide better support for the collection development decision-making process. ERLIC² enhanced access to the full content of ERLIC; adding access to licenses, copies of invoices, and correspondence stored in paper files; improved the reports function; and decreased staff time needed to import, maintain, and export data. The initial ERLIC² design plan also called for development of an online billboard function to alert staff of new trials and the status of access problems. The A-Z list extract could be discontinued as title level access would be generated directly from ERLIC² on a real time basis. Additional data elements were added that followed the data structure then being developed by the Digital Library Federation Electronic Resources Management Initiative (ERMI).

As previously mentioned, one of the goals of ERLIC² was to enhance access to critical documentation. To achieve this goal, an optical imaging database was implemented. Licenses and invoices were scanned, indexed, and linked to the resource records in ERLIC². (See Figure 2 for a graphic representation of the relationship between ERLIC², the image database, and SIRSI Unicorn.)

FIGURE 2. The relationship between ERLIC^2, the image database, and SIRSI Unicorn.

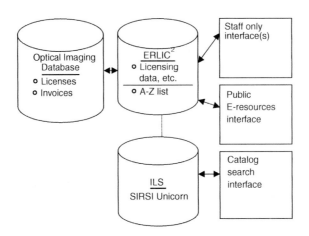

Like many libraries, public access to electronic resources was provided by the A-Z list and online catalog. Penn State Libraries' A-Z list generated from ERLIC^2 provided title level access to all paid electronic resources. The online catalog included both paid and free online resources at the title level or resource level for most full-text aggregations.

The implementation of ERLIC^2 involved migrating ERLIC from Microsoft Access to a Cold Fusion server. ERLIC^2 will eventually be moved to an Oracle platform. Cold Fusion Web pages were developed to access and maintain ERLIC^2.

There were costs attached to ERLIC^2 development. ERLIC^2 required over 300 hours of development and testing. This included approximately 100 pages of code. Migration from ERLIC (Microsoft Access) to ERLIC^2 involved another 300+ hours to review data, key new data, and clean up migrated records and data. Ongoing administration and maintenance of records in both ERLIC and ERLIC^2 require approximately 20-30 hours per week of staff time. This staff commitment did not include time needed for order placement, cataloging, addressing access problems, etc. The commitment of staff resources for ERLIC^2 development was justified based on the need to continue to keep track of content supported by such a significant portion of the collections budget.

ERLIC^2 + VENDOR SOLUTIONS

The landscape has changed since ERLIC was first implemented in 1999. The first change was a change of culture within Penn State Libraries. The need to develop in-house systems was replaced by a need to reallocate staff resources to new initiatives and partner with commercial vendors to develop solutions. Vendors have responded to library market demand for products and services that help keep track of electronic resources and improve content delivery.

In 2002, a task group was charged to examine technological alternatives for content delivery and electronic resource management. As a result of the task group's recommendation, a request for proposal was issued in 2004, and the Libraries acquired Ex Libris's SFX (context sensitive linking) and MetaLib (portal) products in the fall of 2004. (See Figure 3 for a graphic representation of the relationship between ERLIC², SFX, and SIRSI Unicorn.)

The implementation of SFX and MetaLib will eventually impact the role of ERLIC². The A-Z list was generated from title specific entries in ERLIC². Following implementation of SFX, the A-Z list will be generated from the SFX KnowledgeBase. Title level records for full-text aggregations or electronic journal packages may no longer be maintained in ERLIC², but resource records for e-journal packages and full-text aggregations will continue to be maintained. Licenses in the optical imaging database will be linked to resource records in ERLIC².

While content delivery will improve following implementation of SFX, the role of ERLIC² as an analytical tool may diminish. This is because title level records are required for some reports (e.g., comparison of coverage across databases).

Stakeholders continue to require tools, such as ERLIC², that support the collection development decision-making process. However, alternative solutions, including leveraging title level data from the SFX KnowledgeBase and acquisitions data from SIRSI Unicorn, need to be explored.

CONCLUSIONS

Marshall Breeding suggests that there are ". . . two fundamental aspects to managing electronic resources: back-end acquisition functions and front-end content delivery."[5] Penn State Libraries developed ERLIC in 1998/1999 to support some of the back-end acquisition functions and some aspects of front-end content delivery. ERLIC, followed by ERLIC², will continue to manage licensing, authentication, access, ordering, and payment information. The front-end content delivery supported by ERLIC² is no longer necessary, as Penn State Libraries has decided to take advantage of vendor solutions for managing and delivering content.

Many library management system vendors are now developing or planning to develop electronic resource management systems that are either integrated within their systems or will be offered as stand-alone systems. Vendors have indicated that they are modeling their systems based on the data structure pro-

FIGURE 3. The relationship between ERLIC^2, SFX, and SIRSI Unicorn following implementation of SFX.

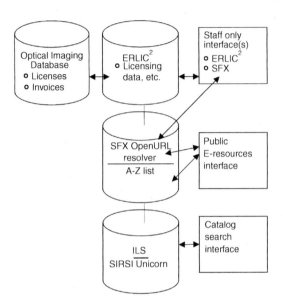

posed by the Digital Library Federation Electronic Resource Management Initiative. This is a very encouraging development for libraries.

Vendors have now developed effective tools for delivering content. However, it is the back-end acquisitions functions that still need to be addressed. Electronic resource management continues to be challenging. In particular, managing the different publisher pricing models has become much more complex. The distinction between print and online has now become less important. It is management of content that is important. Electronic resource management involves not only keeping track of content but also keeping track of costs associated with resources. The system must be much more than a repository for licensing, authentication, access, ordering, and payment information. The system needs to be a powerful management tool that provides stakeholders with the information they need to make informed decisions.

The development of ERLIC and ERLIC^2 was labor intensive but very useful. The true value of in-house development has been the experience gained from identifying functional requirements based on stakeholders' needs. Libraries, like Penn State, that have taken it upon themselves to develop in-house electronic resource management systems have contributed to the development of standards and solutions.

NOTES

1. For more complete listing of in-house electronic resource management system development, consult "A Web Hub for Developing Administrative Metadata for Electronic Resource Management," available electronically at: <http://www.library.cornell.edu/cts/elicensestudy/home.html> (July 21, 2004).

2. Digital Library Federation Electronic Resources Management Initiative submission drafts (July 2004), available electronically at: <http://www.library.cornell.edu/cts/elicensestudy/home.html> (July 21, 2004).

3. A report on workshop presented at 14th NASIG Annual Conference (1999): Cochenour, Donnice. "Taming the Octopus: Getting a Grip on Electronic Resources." *The Serials Librarian.* 38 no. 3-4 (2000): p. 363-368.

4. A report on workshop presented at 17th NASIG Annual Conference (2002): McCaslin, Sharon. "Web-Based Tracking Systems for Electronic Resources Management." *The Serials Librarian.* 44 no. 304 (2003): 293-297.

5. Breeding, Marshall. "The Many Facets of Managing Electronic Resources." *Computers in Libraries.* 24, no. 1 (2004): 25-28.

One-Stop:
Serials Management with TDNet

Peggy S. Cooper
Dan Lester

SUMMARY. The times, they are a-changin'! Serials control continues to be both challenging and complex. Librarians and their patrons can access thousands of journals in a variety of formats and from a variety of starting points. The challenge for Albertsons Library at Boise State University was to meet the needs of the patrons who want only one starting point to access the full-text articles they need. This article describes the process of finding a commercial solution to the problem of one-stop serials management and access. *[Article copies available for a fee from The Haworth Document Delivery Service: 1-800-HAWORTH. E-mail address: <docdelivery@haworthpress.com> Website: <http://www.HaworthPress.com> © 2005 by The Haworth Press, Inc. All rights reserved.]*

KEYWORDS. Serials management, electronic journals, TDNet

Peggy S. Cooper is Coordinator of Collection Development, Albertsons Library, Boise State University, Boise, ID 83725-1430 (E-mail: pcooper@boisestate.edu).

Dan Lester is Network Information Coordinator, Albertsons Library, Boise State University, Boise, ID 83725-1430 (E-mail: dlester@boisestate.edu).

[Haworth co-indexing entry note]: "One-Stop: Serials Management with TDNet." Cooper, Peggy S., and Dan Lester. Co-published simultaneously in *The Serials Librarian* (The Haworth Information Press, an imprint of The Haworth Press, Inc.) Vol. 47, No. 4, 2005, pp. 27-34; and: *Electronic Journal Management Systems: Experiences from the Field* (ed: Gary Ives) The Haworth Information Press, an imprint of The Haworth Press, Inc., 2005, pp. 27-34. Single or multiple copies of this article are available for a fee from The Haworth Document Delivery Service [1-800-HAWORTH, 9:00 a.m. - 5:00 p.m. (EST). E-mail address: docdelivery@haworthpress.com].

That's where all the rest of scholarship starts, Garion. All the books [*serials*] in the world won't help you if they're just piled up in a heap.

–David Eddings, *King of the Murgos*[1]

As we continue to move from a collection-based view to an access-based view of the library, we at Albertsons Library, Boise State University, needed to find a way to manage access to our journals. Although our serials weren't "piled in a heap," access to our complete holdings was complex. Our goal was, and continues to be, to give our users access to the information they need regardless of where that information is located: within a database, on our shelves, or at a publisher's Website, and in whatever format it occurs, paper, microform or emerging e-formats. We wanted to provide our users with a one-stop, coherent interface to diverse journal collections and services. Libraries around the world were also searching for ways to provide the same type of service. We are all dealing with patrons who ". . . wanted to go to our Web site and, with no training and a few magic clicks, get to the full-text article they needed. No two-step, three-step process for them. The Web generation demands full text and they want it now. Don't talk about copyright or passwords. They know it's all technologically possible and they want it NOW."[2]

For over a decade a printed list of serials in the library had been produced and distributed around the building. By late 2000 that list had become unwieldy to produce and outdated as soon as it was printed. In addition, it cost over $9,000 per year in direct costs, plus staff time for pin-binding, to produce the necessary 120 copies three times a year. That list also included none of the titles in aggregator databases, as maintaining such records would have been overwhelming with our limited staff. In addition, the printed list was out of date before bound copies ever reached public service points. For a year we had also used the open-source service jake (Jointly Administered Knowledge Environment, from http://jake.lib.sfu.ca/) to provide information about journals in databases. The printed list and jake were of some assistance, but didn't meet all of our needs. The combination of services required users to check the online catalog, a separate and incomplete e-journal list for individual subscriptions only, a printed list, and jake to determine the availability of a journal title.

We have the technical expertise in the library to design and implement an in-house serials management system; that approach, however, can be very costly in both staff development time and in maintenance. The Herrick Library at Alfred University in Alfred, New York, opted for a locally constructed database, finding in their particular situation that it required a relative small investment in software and hardware. They did report, however, that their process took about six months and "quite a bit of sweat."[3] Although they found that the Herrick Library serials list is easy for their staff to maintain, we were anticipating some staff changes that we thought might complicate both development and long-term maintenance. We also had a serials collection about three times the size of Herrick Library. We decided to take some advice from Michael Gorman's "Five New Laws of Librarianship" and "use technology intelligently to enhance service."[4] Rather than reinvent that technology, we began a search for a commercial vendor that had a serials management product or service already available.

If a suitable commercial product could be located, we would not only be using existing technology intelligently to enhance service but hoped we would also achieve:

1. an accurate representation of ejournals inside aggregator databases;
2. a representation of ejournals that are subscribed to through vendors or directly from publishers, including 'free' journals;
3. a "one stop shopping" list of not only our journals but all of our serial holdings regardless of format; and,
4. usage statistics at the database and title level.

Beginning in the late spring of 2001, a committee composed of the Head of Cataloging, Head of Serials, Network Information Coordinator, and Collection Development Librarian began locating and investigating companies who were marketing ejournals management products. Three vendors were identified at that time: TDNet, JournalWebCite, and Serials Solutions. TDNet, a subsidiary of Teldan Information Systems Limited, an Israeli-based company, was incorporated in the U.S. in February 2001. Serials Solutions was founded by Peter McCracken, Coordinator of Reference Services for the Odegaard Undergraduate Library at the University of Washington, and incorporated in March 2000. Benjamin Adams, of Philadelphia, Pennsylvania, founded JournalWebCite in November 2000. Several other companies have entered the marketplace in the last two years, including EBSCO A-to-Z (http://atoz.ebsco.com), 1cate (http://www.openly.com/1cate/), Journal Finder (http://journalfinder.uncg.edu/), and others. Since our original search for providers JournalWebCite has been purchased by TDNet and Serials Solutions has been purchased by ProQuest.

We identified and talked with customers of TDNet, Serials Solutions, and JournalWebCite, read company literature, visited their Websites, and made numerous conference calls to the various sales representatives. We summarized the information in a comparison chart of the three systems. (See Table 1.) Ellen Finnie Duranceau published a similar summary of the three companies and their services including a comparison chart in her recent article, "E-journal Package-Content Tracking Services."[5]

TDNet offered the broadest range of services and we selected it in October 2001. Although the other two products handled the information on titles in aggregator databases, they didn't provide statistical information on usage of the titles or databases. They also lacked an easy method of integrating locally owned print and microform holdings and were updated less frequently than

TABLE 1. Electronic Journal Management Comparison Chart, Summer 2002

Features	Journal/WebCite	Serials Solutions	TDNet
Coverage display	yes–if more than 1 place, 1 title entry with coverage of all	yes–if more than 1 place, title entry for each	yes–if more than 1 place, title entry for each, or mouse over for each
Customized interface	yes	yes–html or Excel, local	yes–customized to specific collection, logos, local preferences, menu bars
Direct article linking if possible	yes	yes–if possible, approx 65%	yes
Document delivery	?	?	yes
Embaragoed titles		yes–closed holdings statement	will work with us to represent them in the list
Full-text titles	yes	yes	yes
Hosted	their server or ours	our server	their server or ours
Index & Abstract titles	no	no	yes
Licenses	subs based	annual subscription	annual subscription
Links to journal–aggregator	yes	yes	yes–updates urls, tracks appearance/removal of titles, harvests table of contents
Links to journal–free		yes	yes
Links to journal–password	yes	yes–we have to provide url with ISSN which may require a script	yes
Links to journal–print	yes	yes	yes
Links to journal–publisher		yes	yes, if desired
Links to journal–vendor		yes	yes, if desired
Multiple database listings	yes	yes	yes
Number of titles	30,000	160,000	30,000
Records include:			yes–can include title, vendor, publisher, archive, access permissions, print holdings, local view
Remote access	yes	yes	yes
Rpts: Cost comparisons		no	
Rpts: Duplicate coverage	yes	no	yes
Rpts: Use statistics–provider produced	dynamically produced	no	no?
Rpts: Use statistics–library produced	?	no	yes
Rpts: Use statistics–title level	yes	no	yes
Rpts: Use statistics–database level	yes	no	yes
Rpts: Use statistics–breakdown by cost	yes	no	yes?
Rpts: Use statistics–bookmarking	no	no	no
Search engine–site search/title, ISSN	yes	beta testing–2 wks	yes
Search engine–subject	yes–can be locally defined, limited at this time, no boolean	not yet–exploring LC	yes–boolean
Search engine–table of contents	no	no	yes
Set up time–library	approx 1 hr	1 hr	approx 1 hr
Set up time–provider	immediate for databases	2 wks to 1 month	Immediate for databases
Table of contents alerting service	no	no	yes
Table of contents searching	no	no	yes
Updates–frequency	90-day guarantee	can be monthly, otherwise every other month	weekly

TDNet's weekly cycle. We considered frequent updates to be a critical service as databases change on an almost daily basis and we have been fortunate to be able to add new databases on a regular basis. The other products did have the advantage of being considerably less expensive, however. Either of them would have saved in comparison to the printed lists we had been providing instead of costing somewhat more. TDNet also offered the ability to provide weekly current awareness notifications by title or subject for users who had established personal profiles with the MyTDNet service. Finally, readily available statistical reports at the title level were critical for our collection development and analysis procedures.

We originally planned to have the service operating by early November 2001. However, the addition of our locally owned print and microform titles turned out to be more complex than originally anticipated, and there were some difficulties performing the integration. We introduced TDNet to our staff and patrons on January 7, 2002. At the time of our implementation, we were the second site in the U.S. and the only TDNet customer using the database to provide a complete list of all of serials holdings whether in print, microform, or electronic format, current and dead or discontinued titles. Not only were we very happy to see our new serials management system come online but we were also pleased that we were following another of Gorman's New Laws by, in a small way, "helping to create the future."[6] The Boise State University installation's home page is shown here (see Figure 1), and may be seen online at *http://tdnet.boisestate.edu*. The online version is available to anyone with Web access, although access to articles is restricted to those currently affiliated with Boise State University.

At first the service ran from an off-campus site hosted by TDNet in the United States. Since we prefer to manage our own services whenever possible, and since we were experienced with Microsoft SQL Server 2000 and Windows 2000 Server, we later moved the installation to one of the servers in the library. The nine-hour time difference and the different work weeks provided a few communication problems, but they were resolved quickly. We continue to work closely with the TDNet staff to add, delete, and correct title records in our list of serials and to request and monitor changes in the databases. This takes more staff time than we initially anticipated but still takes considerably less time than if we had developed a local system or had added electronic resources to our printed list.

The TDNet serials management system, which we call simply the Journals List, has been extremely popular at our library. Our faculty, students, and staff are pleased with the one-stop access to all of our serials information from the Journals List. Faculty members and graduate students are happy with the weekly table of contents alerting service, MyTDNet. Once a subscriber has created an account, weekly alerting notices are sent directly to his or her e-mail address. This was not on our original list of requirements for a serials management system but has been a welcomed addition and was a factor in our

FIGURE 1. Opening Screen of TDNet at Boise State University Albertsons Library

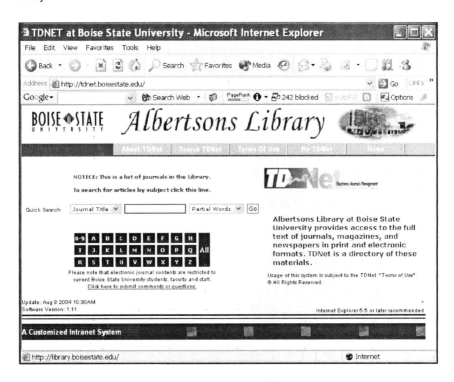

selection of this service. The direct links to the content of ejournals have greatly increased the usage of these resources. We can access usage information on a title by title basis from staff computers at any time. Since Boise State has a great many distance education students, providing services to students around the world is vital to the library. We are able to provide the full electronic resources of the library to all of our users, by the use of EZProxy to connect remote users. TDNet staff has facilitated the use of EZProxy for our technical staff by also providing weekly updates to the configuration file that software uses. This updated file from TDNet has greatly simplified maintenance of the EZProxy server for us.

We have been very pleased with the excellent customer service that we have received from TDNet. We work closely with the sales staff, the technical support group, and the President of the company and have found that they are extremely attentive to customer input and suggestions. They have made numerous changes to the database based on that input. Some examples for those changes in the past year are true word searching, removing unnecessary icons, and adding a quick search box.

Augustine Birrell pointed out more than a century ago that libraries are not made; they grow.[7] We expect our library and our serials management system to continue to grow and improve. One particular improvement we are hoping for in the near future is better subject searching. Subject searching is not the strongest feature in TDNet. This has not been a significant problem for us to date, as we do not encourage patrons to use the Journals List for that purpose. Although improved subject searching capabilities would be useful, the primary purpose of the serials management system at Albertsons Library is to give access to specific, known titles. Subject/article searches should begin in the subject appropriate database, such as *America History and Life* or *ERIC*. The results of those searches should then be checked in the Journals List.

One of the most recent developments in TDNet has been the addition of their TDNet Open URL Resolver, TOUR. We've been testing TOUR by adding TOUR links to some of our databases so that when a patron finds an article of interest he or she can click on the TOUR links, and in many cases go directly to the article that is on a publisher's Website or in some other aggregator database. Although all Open URL resolvers have problems due to the lack of consistency of linking methods among various databases and publishers, this new feature has facilitated patrons' accessing articles. As standards continue to develop in the Open URL resolver field, this feature will become ever more important in libraries.

Judith Szilvassy wrote in the Foreword of the *Basic Serials Management Handbook* that the management, acquisition and preservation of serials create substantial challenges for librarians.[8] We couldn't agree more. What have we learned from this process? Perhaps it isn't what we learned but rather what was reinforced, something we, Michael Gorman, Judith Szilvassy, and Bob Dylan already knew, that the times, they are a-changin'. Serials control is a challenging and complex business and those challenges and complexity have only been exacerbated with the addition of electronic journals. Albertsons Library's acquisition of TDNet's serials management system is helping the library staff and its patrons to deal with those challenges.

A library starting to search for a serials management system will need to assess their own local needs, and determine which features are essential and which are optional or desirable. A first step would be to review the volatile marketplace as it stands at that time. As more serials management systems vendors enter and leave the business and additional services become available, we would recommend asking at least the following questions from any vendor before purchasing a system.

1. What are the essential features of your serials management system?
2. What are the costs for the initial system?
3. What are the costs for continuing operation and maintenance?

4. What is the estimated amount of time from contract signing to live system?
5. How frequently will system updates be made?
6. Where will the system be hosted?
7. Can your vendor provide additional services beyond the A-Z list?
8. Do you want or need additional serials management services?
   • Full or brief catalog records
   • Notification of changes in titles in the system
   • Table of contents alerting service
   • Open URL Link Resolver
   • Federated searching over all electronic databases and the online catalog
   • Statistical reports on usage of titles and databases

In addition, those investigating the acquisition of a serials management system should be sure to consult with comparable libraries that are actually using the various systems under consideration. As the marketplace changes and systems develop, merge, and die, some libraries will change their serials system provider for various reasons. The researcher should be sure to contact a variety of users, and not just those to which they are referred by the prospective vendor.

NOTES

1. David Eddings, *King of the Murgos*. New York: Ballantine Books, 1987.
2. Davida Scharf, "Interim Serials Management Strategies from the Real Virtual World," *Searcher* 8, no.2 (2000): 59-64.
3. Gary Roberts, "Constructing a Database of Local Serials Holdings," *Computers in Libraries* 19, no.9 (1999): 24-35.
4. Michael Gorman, "Five New Laws of Librarianship," *American Libraries* 26, no.8 (1995): 784-785.
5. Ellen Finnie Duranceau, "E-journal Package-Content Tracking Services," *Serials Review* 28, no.1 (2002): 49-52.
6. Gorman, "Five New Laws of Librarianship," 784-785.
7. Augustine Birrell, *Obiter Dicta*. New York: C. Scribner's sons, 1885.
8. Judith Szilvassy, *Basic Serials Management Handbook*. New Providence [N.J.]: K.G. Saur, 1996.

Taming the E-Journal Jungle: The University of South Carolina's Experience with TDNet

Karen McMullen

Derek Wilmott

SUMMARY. The University of South Carolina libraries experienced a sudden increase in the number of electronic journals to add to the libraries' collections. A library committee selected the TDNet e-journal management system, due to specific academic and economic needs, to organize the ever-growing e-journal collection. The focus of this article is to describe the selection process and the current use of the TDNet e-journal management service in the USC Libraries system. *[Article copies available for a fee from The Haworth Document Delivery Service: 1-800-HAWORTH. E-mail address: <docdelivery@haworthpress.com> Website: <http://www.HaworthPress.com> © 2005 by The Haworth Press, Inc. All rights reserved.]*

Karen McMullen is Serials Acquisitions Librarian, Thomas Cooper Library, University of South Carolina. She holds a BA in Special Education from Columbia College and an MLIS from the University of South Carolina (E-mail: Karen.McMullen@sc.edu).

Derek Wilmott is Serials Cataloging Librarian, Thomas Cooper Library, University of South Carolina. He holds a BA in Psychology and a Bachelor's in Criminal Justice from New Mexico State University and an MLIS from the University of South Carolina (E-mail: wilmott@sc.edu).

Address correspondence to the authors at: Thomas Cooper Library, University of South Carolina, Columbia, SC 29208.

[Haworth co-indexing entry note]: "Taming the E-Journal Jungle: The University of South Carolina's Experience with TDNet." McMullen, Karen, and Derek Wilmott. Co-published simultaneously in *The Serials Librarian* (The Haworth Information Press, an imprint of The Haworth Press, Inc.) Vol. 47, No. 4, 2005, pp. 35-42; and: *Electronic Journal Management Systems: Experiences from the Field* (ed: Gary Ives) The Haworth Information Press, an imprint of The Haworth Press, Inc., 2005, pp. 35-42. Single or multiple copies of this article are available for a fee from The Haworth Document Delivery Service [1-800-HAWORTH, 9:00 a.m. - 5:00 p.m. (EST). E-mail address: docdelivery@haworthpress.com].

KEYWORDS. Electronic journals, electronic journal management systems, management systems, TDNet, University of South Carolina

INTRODUCTION

Electronic resources have changed the way librarians meet the information needs of their clientele. The move to electronic resources has touched all areas within the library organization. Collection Development officers are looking at e-journals as a method to solve space needs by removing print publications from the shelves. Reference librarians are educating faculty and students to use e-resources. Acquisition librarians are wrestling with the purchasing and licensing of electronic-based products. Cataloging and systems librarians are devising methods for library users to access electronic resources in both the online catalog and through their organization's Web pages. The move from print to electronic formats has added a new level of complexity for Serials Librarians, creating an electronic jungle, as they struggle to meet user access needs. One major problem with e-journals is they are packaged differently, depending on the publishers and vendors. Some vendors provide collections by discipline as in the case with Science Direct and JSTOR titles. Others, such as Lexis Nexis, are sold within aggregated databases. So how do librarians tame the e-journal jungle? Here at the University of South Carolina (USC), the decision was made to use TDNet, a commercial e-journal management system to resolve the issue.

THE SETTING

USC is a public institution composed of a main campus and seven branch campuses located throughout the state. The University has more than 34,500 students and approximately 2,000 faculty on the eight campuses. The primary mission of the University is to serve the educational needs of the citizens of South Carolina through teaching, research, service, and creative activity. USC houses eight libraries on the main campus and seven additional libraries at the branch campuses. The primary mission of the USC libraries is to acquire, organize, and promote the use of scholarly collections supporting the educational, research, and service missions at USC.

SELECTION PROCESS

In the past few years, it became apparent that the e-journal collections at USC were growing at a phenomenal rate and could no longer be maintained by adding titles to both the online catalog (USCAN) and to the library's Web pages. None of the titles in the aggregator databases were represented in USCAN, Electronic Indexes, or the Science Library's Web pages. The Science Reference librarian and several student assistants had developed an e-journals Web page for the sciences which quickly expanded to include e-journals from the humanities and social sciences. It soon became clear that this e-journal environment was becoming a jungle that needed taming. The Science Reference Librarian and the student assistants were no longer able to maintain URLs and update titles to the publisher databases on the Science Library's Web pages.

A committee was formed, with representatives from Reference, Collection Development, Cataloging, Systems, Acquisitions, and the Science Library to review the available methods of e-journal management. The committee realized that there were few options available to adequately manage e-journal collections. In an e-mail correspondence, dated June 23, 2004, Gail Julian, former Serials Acquisitions Librarian at the Thomas Cooper Library (TCL) said that a proprietary service offered the best solution to managing the e-journal collections at USC. After careful consideration, TDNet was selected to handle the e-journal collections for all the USC libraries, with the exception of the Law School Library. The committee recommended TDNet because it could list all the titles within the aggregator databases and could also provide usage statistics, subject access, the ability to accommodate a library consortium, and Z39.50 links to USCAN.

One of the main selling points that impressed the committee was TDNet's ability to provide access to individual titles within aggregator databases. This function greatly enhanced the level of library user access and overall awareness of the titles, which were usually "invisible" within the databases. A concern of some librarians was that many of the titles within the aggregator databases were going unnoticed by the academic community, possibly due to its lack of understanding of how these types of resources worked. Other issues of concern were usage statistics within these aggregator databases. In late October 2002, TCL, the seven branch campus libraries, and the School of Medicine Library signed a contract with TDNet to provide the much needed management of the e-journal collections.

TDNET E-JOURNAL MANAGEMENT SERVICE

What is TDNet? According to Michael Markwith, President of TDNet Inc., in a 2001 interview, TDNet is an e-journal management and access service which allows librarians and their libraries to retain local control while providing full and complete Web access to their e-content. (Flowers, 2001) At present, there are a number of electronic journal management systems available to libraries needing to control their e-journals collections. Michelle Sitko et al. and Ellen Finnie Duranceau provide excellent descriptions of electronic journal management systems available to libraries by each of the proprietary-based products in their articles in *Serials Review*.

The TDNet e-journal management system created by TDNet Ltd (http://www.tdnet.com/) was launched in August 2000. The company is a subsidiary of Teldan Information Systems, Ltd. (http://www.teldan.com/TelDan/index.asp), headquartered in Tel Aviv, Israel. The TDNet e-journal management system was purchased in the fall of 2000 by participating member libraries at USC to provide management and access to the current e-journal collections, including online newspapers. In an e-mail correspondence, on July 13, 2004, Michael Markwith states that "TDNet is used by over 500 libraries in the United States (counting consortia members as separate libraries) and over 1,000 libraries worldwide . . . 80% are academic, 10% medical, 5% federal, and 5% corporate."

At the time of writing this article there are over 65,000 electronic journal Websites, 35,000 Table of Contents records, and over 500 databases available through this service. Access to all e-journal titles within TDNet is located in TCL, which acts as the clearinghouse for electronic journal collections purchased individually or as part of a larger, aggregator service. This system works as part of an integrated electronic journal collection, for USC and the branch campus libraries. USCAN (http://www.sc.edu/uscan) and the Electronic Indexes Web page (http://www.sc.edu/library/ei.html) are the other two access points for the USC academic community. Presently, the USC libraries have approximately 20,000 titles available through TDNet, with new titles added weekly.

The Acquisitions Department at TCL assisted in setting up accounts with TDNet for all participating libraries. The Head of Acquisitions compiled lists of titles from the aggregator databases so that individual libraries could customize their e-journal collections on their TDNet Web pages. The Serials Acquisitions Unit manages usage statistics reports available in the TDNet Administrative Module. The listing of all e-journal titles in one location creates a level of overlap between library collections primarily due to licensing agreements. For the most part, access is available to most e-journals; there are exceptions with a few titles that have access restrictions for a specific library. For example, EBSCO Business Source Premier is available for use only at the Business Library. Access notes and other information relevant to a specific title are added and maintained by the Serials Acquisitions Unit.

TAMING THE JUNGLE WITH TDNET

There are three ways to access TDNet at USC. Each library's Web page has a banner with hyperlinks to specific resources, including one entitled, "E-Journals," that takes users directly to TDNet's e-journal management system.

A second access point is through the Electronic Indexes Web page. The third access point is through TCL's Web page, listed under the "Resources" link.

The following scenario is a hypothetical search method. A researcher could first conduct a search using an online index located on TCL's Electronic Indexes Web page to locate citations or full-text articles. After locating a citation, the search continues using TDNet, either by searching for a specific title or by using the TDNet Open URL Resolver to link to a full-text article. If the citation is not available electronically, the user has the option of using USCAN to locate a print version of the publication. If it is determined, in the course of the search, that USC libraries does not have access to the article, the researcher can use the interlibrary loan service or purchase the article directly from the publisher.

The above hypothetical search method is similar to the way patrons used to conduct research before libraries automated. In the "old days," libraries maintained both print listings and a card catalog of journals in a collection. The researcher could look through the journal lists for a specific title, utilize the various print indexes and abstracts to search for citations relevant to their topic, or locate individual journal titles using the card catalog. Search habits have incorporated newer technology, but the basic search behaviors remain the same.

The TDNet Website is available to all USC students, faculty, and staff. There are some access limitations, due to subscription licensing agreements with various publishers as to which journal titles are available to the various libraries. There are alternatives for researchers to retrieve articles, such as interlibrary loan or purchasing individual articles directly from the publisher. These alternatives are subject to the perceived importance (i.e., time, cost, or other limiting factors) placed on retrieving the journal articles by the researcher.

TDNet is modular, meaning libraries may choose which types of services they wish to purchase. The four services that can be purchased separately, or as parts of an integrated e-content solution are:

1. TDNet E-Journal Management (EJM)
2. TDNet eContent Searcher (TES)*
3. TDNet Catalog Maintenance Service (CMS)*
4. TDNet Open URL Resolver (TOUR)

*USC Libraries does not subscribe to these features at this time.

TDNet E-Journal Management (EJM), a Web-based A-Z list of full-text e-journals, is available in two versions, TDNet Management Links and TDNet Complete. USC libraries purchased TDNet Complete. This module features an alphabetized list of journal titles, online coverage, vendor/database information, print holdings which link to USCAN, and Table of Contents (TOC).

The EJM module is updated on a weekly basis and requires maintenance by the Serials Acquisitions Unit using the administrative functions.

Each library has the option of customizing its main TDNet Web page to fit its needs. The Electronic Information Products Team at TCL customized the TDNet Web page as seen in Figure 1, with links to the USC libraries' main homepage and USCAN. Other changes to the main Web page include a TDNet Help link, which is an abbreviated user's guide. An Off-Campus Access link assists users in accessing electronic resources using a proxy server. A search feature allows a library patron to search by journal title, ISSN, publisher, or vendor. A browsing feature of all titles is available on the main page using the A-Z list, which is library specific. Two service buttons were also created. The first button labeled, "Ask a Librarian," allows a user with an e-mail account to submit questions to a reference librarian. The second button directs users to the interlibrary loan ordering system at USC. There is a free-text area where information is tailored to each specific library. Every customized version of the TDNet home page has standard buttons: About TDNet, Search TDNet, Terms of Use, and My TDNet. The Administrator Login link allows an autho-

FIGURE 1. TDNet Main Page for TCL

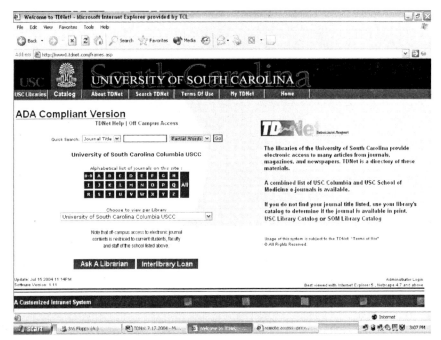

rized user to customize the interface by adding journal note messages, making changes to titles, and creating usage statistics reports.

TDNet Open URL Resolver (TOUR) became available to users in the fall of 2003. It is based on Open URL rules and is NISO Standard Compliant. TOUR consists of five components:

1. A resource database, which contains information about the library's licensed resources
2. A holdings database, which contains information about specific on-line coverage dates
3. Link resolving
4. User interface functions
5. Administrator interface functions

When TOUR is used in conjunction with TDNet EJM and TDNet TES, the link resolver allows the user to link to almost any online resource. No additional input is required from the library in terms of maintaining holdings data, and no additional server is required. So far, only a few databases at TCL have been activated using the TOUR modules.

The TOUR module (Figure 2) is still in its infancy at TCL. As of spring 2004, TCL has activated ten databases and the branch campus libraries have activated two databases. One of the more important features of TOUR is the user interface function. This feature allows a researcher to search in an abstract or index database (i.e., Cambridge Scientific Abstracts) with a hyperlink titled, "Check for full text access," which in turn will direct a user to the journal title in TDNet. There are a few limitations to this feature, such as the availability to a full-text source. The researcher then has the option of searching USCAN for a print version, requesting the article through interlibrary loan, or purchasing the article from the publisher. It is still too early to properly gauge the impact TOUR is making, but it will be interesting to see what the user response will be when more of the USC library community is aware of its capabilities.

CONCLUSION

TDNet has had a positive impact within the USC library community. There has been closer collaboration of the Reference, Serials Acquisitions and Cataloging staffs in an effort to provide greater access and education to the library community in using the e-resource collections. Some areas need improvement, such as providing enhanced user information in the "My TDNet" page and adding a link directly to the TDNet User's Guide located on the USC Electronic Indexes Web page. Taming the e-journal jungle is a long and arduous process, requiring creative solutions such as TDNet's e-journal management system.

FIGURE 2. TDNet TOUR Results in Cambridge Scientific Abstracts for the Journal *Phi Delta Kappan*

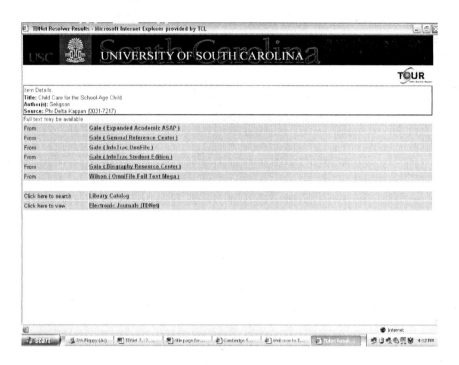

REFERENCES

Duranceau, Ellen Finnie. "E-journal Package-Content Tracking Services." *Serials Review* 28, no. 1 (spring 2002): 49-52

Flowers, Janet L. "ATG Interviews Michael Markwith," *Against the Grain* 13, no. 3 (June 2001): 42-46

Sitko, Michelle, Narda Tafuri, Gregory Szczyrbak, and Taemin Park. "E-journal Management Systems: Trends, Trials, and Trade-offs." *Serials Review* 28, no. 3 (Autumn 2002): 176-194

Implementing EBSCO's A-to-Z and LinkSource Products for Improved Electronic Journal Management

Virginia A. Lingle

SUMMARY. As the acquisition of electronic resources continued to grow at the George T. Harrell Library, so too did the need for automated management of the links to those resources, for better tracking of changes in coverage, and for a more efficient compilation of usage statistics for collection development. Several products were tested and in May 2004, the EBSCO A-to-Z and LinkSource products were purchased as part of a package that included several full-text databases. This article will discuss why the EBSCO products were selected; what was done to prepare for the implementation process; how the transition was made from a static A-to-Z Web list of journals; and what are the benefits and challenges of using the EBSCO products to date. *[Article copies available for a fee from The Haworth Document Delivery Service: 1-800-HAWORTH. E-mail address: <docdelivery@haworthpress.com> Website:*

Virginia A. Lingle, MSLS, is Librarian, Serials and Cataloging, George T. Harrell Library, Milton S. Hershey Medical Center, Pennsylvania State University College of Medicine, 500 University Drive, Hershey, PA 17033-0850 (E-mail: val3@psu.edu).

The author wishes to express thanks to Chris Gorman (CGorman@epnet.com) and Rob Depaolo (RDepaolo@epnet.com) of the EBSCO company for their assistance with the preparation of this article. The EBSCO Information Services Web site is located at www.ebsco.com.

[Haworth co-indexing entry note]: "Implementing EBSCO's A-to-Z and LinkSource Products for Improved Electronic Journal Management." Lingle, Virginia A. Co-published simultaneously in *The Serials Librarian* (The Haworth Information Press, an imprint of The Haworth Press, Inc.) Vol. 47, No. 4, 2005, pp. 43-54; and: *Electronic Journal Management Systems: Experiences from the Field* (ed: Gary Ives) The Haworth Information Press, an imprint of The Haworth Press, Inc., 2005, pp. 43-54. Single or multiple copies of this article are available for a fee from The Haworth Document Delivery Service [1-800-HAWORTH, 9:00 a.m. - 5:00 p.m. (EST). E-mail address: docdelivery@haworthpress.com].

Digital Object Identifier: 10.1300/J123v47n04_06

KEYWORDS. EBSCO, A-to-Z, LinkSource, electronic journal management, link resolver

INTRODUCTION

The George T. Harrell Library is the primary resource library for the College of Medicine and the Milton S. Hershey Medical Center of The Pennsylvania State University. Located in South Central Pennsylvania, the College of Medicine is a separate campus situated two hours south of the main university and has its own budget administration. There are about 7,000 employees at the campus, which include more than 400 clinical and research faculty, and more than 550 medical and graduate students in the life sciences. The Library's mission states that it is "committed to providing instruction and access to informational resources and services in support of the needs of faculty, students, and staff engaged in patient care, research, and education and to extending these resources and services, in so far as possible, to the biomedical community throughout the Commonwealth of Pennsylvania and beyond." With the current economy, as budgets grow tighter and the demand for resources continue to increase, the Library had to seek more efficient ways to fulfill that mission and to provide what users needed.

Four years ago, in an effort to better utilize existing monies, the first of several contracts was negotiated with the University Libraries at main campus to include access to numerous electronic resources for the Harrell Library users. Additional contracts were negotiated for access to resources that are unique to the Harrell Library, which brought the total number of access points to over 10,000 links to maintain on static Web pages with an A-to-Z type of list. The management of electronic journal access information became an impossible task to handle manually with 1 FTE; neither could statistics on the use of the electronic resources be efficiently gathered and tabulated.

For these reasons, several commercial products for electronic journal management were reviewed including those developed by OVID, TDNET, Serials Solutions, SIRSI, and others. It is not the intent of this article to compare these products; but instead, the purpose is to discuss why the EBSCO products were chosen. The Harrell Library was already an EBSCO customer for journal orders for two years and had received excellent service with that branch of the company. There was an existing account for the library, and EBSCO knew which print titles were being acquired and which of the titles included electronic access. Because several full-text databases were also being considered for purchase, a discounted price for the electronic journal management products was negotiated that made EBSCO very competitive. EBSCO would host the system at the company site, which for a library with a staff of only 14 people, also was a benefit. In the final selection, the factors that decided the purchase decision included the fact that the company was very reputable, provided excellent service in other areas, negotiated a very competitive price, and had products that seemed to be easy to implement and use.

"WHERE TO START?"

Once the contract was signed and the invoice was paid, the several-month trial access was converted to a subscription with full customer support. Since several modules were purchased at the same time, the biggest challenge, initially, was to more completely understand how the different modules interacted with each other, what features were available in each, and how customizing settings in one module would impact on what was displayed to users in the other modules. It took some time to become familiar with the terminology used by the EBSCO company. To illustrate how some of the confusion could occur, below is a list of the EBSCO products to which the Harrell Library currently has access with descriptions taken from the EBSCO documentation.

EBSCONet® is EBSCO's Web-based serials management system that allows administrators to order, search, claim and renew periodicals from EBSCO's extensive database of more than 282,000 serial titles. This is the business system for managing journal subscriptions.

EBSCOhost is EBSCO's online platform or service from which users can search various databases and link to other resources such as electronic journals, document delivery services, and the library catalog. An accompanying administrative module, called *EBSCOadmin*, allows customers to customize the *EBSCOhost* interface and generate statistical reports depicting usage of the subscribed services.

EJS Basic. The *Electronic Journal Service Basic* interface allows users to directly search and access the full text of electronic journals for which they have subscriptions through EBSCO without the purchase of another database. The *Enhanced* service also allows users to generate usage reports, store user passwords, and do customized branding.

LinkSource is EBSCO's OpenURL link resolver software that provides centralized access to Web-based resources whether purchased through EBSCO or not. A menu of all of the access options for a citation is created based on policies set by the library. When profiles are established with other suppliers, users can start a search with any database service that the library provides and be connected to any subscribed resource no matter where it resides. For non-full-text items, users can be directed to the library catalog, to a serials list, to an interlibrary loan request form, or to a document delivery order form.

A-to-Z Service is the product that provides users with a single, comprehensive list of titles to which they have access. Information on both print and electronic journals can be included. Users can search by keyword, browse an alphabetical list, or search by subjects based on Library of Congress terminology. A companion administrative module also allows for customization of many features, which will be discussed later in this article.

Medline on EBSCOhost. Created by the National Library of Medicine, MEDLINE allows users to search abstracts from over 4,600 current biomedical journals. This database is updated each week.

Academic Search Elite database. This multidisciplinary database offers full text for nearly 2,050 scholarly journals, including nearly 1,500 peer-reviewed titles. Covering virtually every area of academic study, it offers full text information dating as far back as 1985. This database is updated on a daily basis via EBSCOhost.

Health Business FullTEXT Elite database. This database provides full-text coverage for nearly 460 well-known administrative journals. It provides comprehensive journal content detailing all aspects of health care administration and other non-clinical aspects of health care institution management. This database is updated on a daily basis.

Alt HealthWatch database. This alternative health database provides full text for more than 140 publications in the collection, including full text for many peer-reviewed journals. It provides in-depth coverage across the full spectrum of subject areas covered by complementary and alternative medicine dating back to 1990.

American Humanities Index. Produced by Whitston Publishing, this database is a collection of bibliographic references to literary, scholarly and creative journals published in the United States and Canada. It contains over 1,000 journals published from 1975 to the present and was included in the negotiated package at no additional cost.

Communications and Mass Media Complete database. This database provides the most robust, quality research solution in areas related to communication and mass media. It originated with the acquisition and subsequent merging of two popular databases in the fields of communication and mass media studies–CommSearch (formerly produced by the National Communication Association [NCA], and Mass Media Articles Index (formerly produced by Pennsylvania State University). Communication and Mass Media Complete provides an invaluable resource for students, researchers, and educators interested in any and all aspects of communication and mass media. This database was also included at no additional charge in the negotiated package.

There are many other services that EBSCO provides and terms that are used such as TOC Premier, EBSCO SmartLinks, A-to-Z with MARC updates, and other databases such as AMED, SPORTDiscus, and EBSCO Book Services, so it is not surprising that it can be confusing to understand what features and services one is buying with each subscription. This article will focus on the products purchased by the Harrell Library that are most closely related to electronic journal management–the A-to-Z Service and LinkSource.

CUSTOMER SUPPORT

An essential factor in the purchase of any software or online product should be the level of customer support that is available from the company. EBSCO provides this service in several forms.

Web casts. Before the purchase of the software was final, staff could attend, individually or as a group, interactive online demonstrations of products on their desktop using WebEx technology.

On-site training. After the purchase, technical staff from EBSCO visited the campus and conducted hands-on training of how to configure and use the products. Visits were also made before the purchase to demonstrate the *EBSCOhost* interface and database searching features.

Personnel to help with setup and data input. EBSCO technical staff could pull data from the existing static Web pages on the Harrell Library Web site and convert much of the data for input into the A-to-Z service. Help was also provided with settings for proxy access to titles and with the configuration information for the activation of LinkSource with the other database services used by the Harrell Library.

Phone and e-mail contacts. If there is any negative aspect of EBSCO's customer service, it would be that, at times, there were too many contacts made by too many different people. Initially, phone calls and e-mails were so prolific that it was sometimes unclear who the people were and why they were making the contact. With time, the process narrowed to fewer contacts made by a select group of people. It is more helpful to be able to discuss problems and questions with one or two people who know the history of the library's situation.

Web-based tutorials and documentation. The support pages of the EBSCO Web site are freely accessible to any Internet user at <support.epnet.com>. No ID or password is needed except to generate "Title Change Reports." The Web-based support is excellent with features such as a "Spotlight of Top Stories"; online training "Tea Time" which are interactive 20-minute online meetings about EBSCO services; well-designed tutorials on searching, customizing modules, and new products; up-to-date title lists for each database on EBSCOhost; support documentation such as user's guides, setup checklists for products, and how to create an online ILL form. The support site also includes release notes, and a communications archives of recent e-mails that have been globally sent to customers. A user can "open a case" for problem resolution or use "live chat" assistance during business hours. There is also a "Knowledge Base" of FAQs that can be searched for brief answers to inquiries. Figure 1 illustrates the retrieval from a search for proxy information in the A-to-Z module.

Help buttons. Online help options come in several forms with the EBSCO products. The EBSCOhost products have a help button that leads to an extensive file of information on such topics as searching techniques, how to save, view, or print a search, creating a bibliography, or setting options for a user profile. The A-to-Z product uses an "About This Site" tab that leads to sample screens highlighting various features for the user.

IMPLEMENTATION OF THE A-TO-Z SERVICE

Customization

Before any work is done to enter the library's journal holdings into the A-to-Z list, decisions should be made about how the page should look and what data elements are to be included in the list. EBSCO staff can set up the appropriate links to the subscribed products and establish the IP authentication and login codes for access to both the public and administrative pages. The "Administrator" site of A-to-Z allows library staff to manage the journal list, customize the "look and feel" of the public pages (branding), manage links and proxy settings, and generate usage reports.

Branding

Branding options include such features as applying the library logo to the top of pages and entering contact information, such as a phone number or e-

FIGURE 1. Search Screen for the EBSCO Knowledge Base

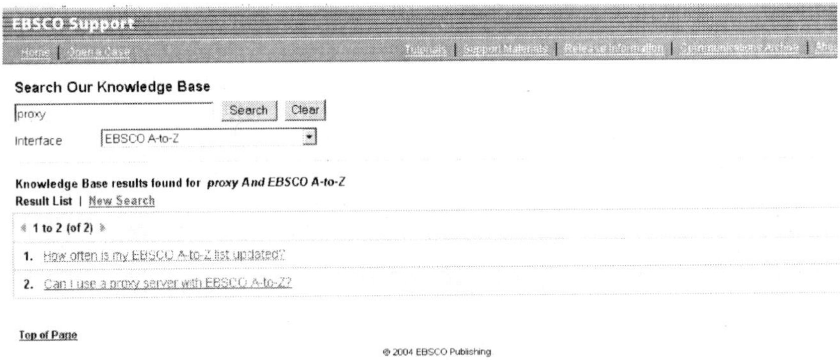

mail address, in a page footer. Brief display messages can be added such as a link to the library's home page or a note that subject categories are based on the Library of Congress system. Various choices can be made about the display of ISSN numbers, subject terms, or publisher information. The number of titles to display per page can easily be modified, as well as can the color and font of each of the text elements on the public pages. Choices can be made to include various search options on the A-to-Z list such as a search button, a link for advanced searching, or a "drop-down" list of titles per page within that range of the alphabet. Libraries can choose to display a secondary alphabetic list by the first two letters of the initial word of a journal title; or to just use page numbers to navigate through long lists of titles. Various "tabs" can easily be set to display or be removed. An "Index" tab leads to a list of the journal providers selected through the Title Maintenance Wizard; a "Subjects" tab displays a hierarchy of subject terms with the number of titles assigned those terms; a "Search" tab allows searching for journal title information by various parameters including ISSNs or publisher; an "About This Site" tab gives explanations of each feature in the A-to-Z list; and a "Titles" tab leads users back to the alphabetic title list itself. A convenient feature is that at any time while making changes in the administrative module, one click on a link to the "Reader's Site" allows for an immediate view of how the edit appears to the user. Figure 2 shows an example of some of the style decisions that were made for the public display of the A-to-Z list at the Harrell Library.

FIGURE 2. Sample of Display Options

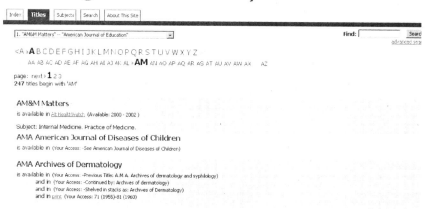

Title List Maintenance

Title list maintenance, at the time of this writing, is done through the downloading, editing, and uploading of a tab-delimited spreadsheet. In the near future, library staff may be able to directly edit data on the system. The current process, to download and upload a spreadsheet, is very easy and edits can be viewed immediately. The biggest challenge, however, with this stage of the implementation is the formatting of the initial list of journal holdings to match the data elements required for EBSCO's data load process. The data elements that are preferred, but are not necessarily all required for an upload include: (1) a resource ID number; (2) the journal title; (3) the format of how the title should be listed alphabetically if different from the main title listing; (4) the full text supplier; (5) the URL; (6) the publisher; (7) the ISSN for the online version of the journal; (8) the ISSN for the print version of the journal; (9) the date that the journal coverage begins; (10) the date that the journal coverage ends or if left blank, the system will supply the word "present;" and (11) an indication of whether the title is to be automatically maintained by EBSCO or manually maintained by the library. EBSCO's pricing tier for A-to-Z is partially based on the number of titles for which EBSCO must maintain the data versus the number of titles or lines of data that are maintained by the library. There are a number of reasons, that will be mentioned later, as to why a library must maintain the data instead of it being managed automatically by the A-to-Z service.

To begin the creation of a master title list of data, the A-to-Z product includes a "Title Maintenance Wizard" function that can be used to quickly add titles. With this "wizard," a user with an administrative password for a library account can select groups of titles by aggregator, by subsets of journals, or by individual titles that are prelisted in the system. When selected, these titles will automatically be included on a master list with all of the necessary data elements. When downloaded, the file can then be reviewed for any edits.

There are several challenges with editing this master list or spreadsheet. A significant amount of staff time may be required for the preparation of the initial load of titles, depending on the size of the library's journal collection, because of the various types of editing that may need to be done to exactly reflect the library's holdings. Another challenge is that even though a library may subscribe to titles through an aggregator, not all of the available titles may have been purchased. When a group of titles from an aggregator listed in the Title Maintenance Wizard is checked, then the entire package is added to the master list. The titles that are not valid subscriptions must then be marked for deletion in the next upload. Also, the start date for an electronic subscription listed in the Title Maintenance Wizard may not match the actual start date in a library's subscription. The start date may differ depending on what was negotiated between the library and the publisher. This change must be edited on the master list for uploading; however, any time that information supplied by the

Title Maintenance Wizard is changed, several steps must be taken. First, the line with the existing information must be marked for deletion on the master list; secondly, a new line of data must be entered for the title with the necessary changes. Any change–whether it is a different date range for holdings, or a spelling correction, or a change in punctuation, or an addition of a special note–will necessitate a new line of data on the spreadsheet. The easiest way to create the new line of data is to copy the existing line generated by the Title Maintenance Wizard and then make the edits. The more information that is supplied about a title, such as an ISSN, etc., the better the system will make the proper match to apply the changes. Unfortunately, when any change is made to data that is system supplied from the Title Maintenance Wizard, the title is no longer automatically managed by the A-to-Z product, but becomes a "custom title" and must be maintained by the library.

Special notes about a title, such as a shelving note or information about the previous title or a continuing title when there are title changes, are not easily entered into the A-to-Z list. A separate line must be entered on the upload spreadsheet for any special notations about a title. As a result, a title may be listed on the spreadsheet many times–for each online access point with date ranges, for each special note about the title, and for print holdings. Figure 2 shows a title with special notes. Figure 3 shows a title with multiple online accesses and date ranges listed.

Each line of information that displays on the A-to-Z list requires a separate line of information on the spreadsheet or master list that is used for uploading

FIGURE 3. Example of Multiple Lines of Access Information for a Title

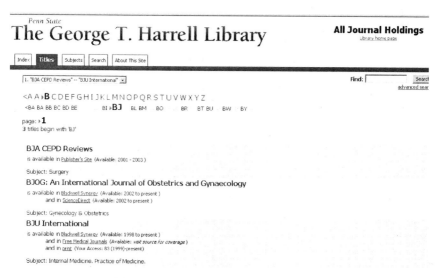

data to the EBSCO server. Titles that are available only in a print format can be listed with a link to the library's catalog for additional information. EBSCO personnel gave the Harrell Library exceptional assistance with this tedious process by converting and uploading the special notes with many of the existing titles from the library's former static A-to-Z title list.

Proxy Access

The A-to-Z module has an automatic proxy URL generator that can be set up to attach the URL for a journal site to the prefix for the library's proxy server. Check boxes allow a library to use a proxy address for "Resource Links"–all links on the A-to-Z list; for "Custom Links"–titles with modified data that are input by the library; or for "Index Links"–those titles that are part of aggregation packages subscribed to by the library and indicated in the "Title Maintenance Wizard." EBSCO staff removed the proxy prefix from any title that did not allow proxy access by contract and from any title that is freely accessible across the Internet.

Usage Reports

The Usage Reports module on the A-to-Z Administrator site is very easy to use and quickly generates tables in tab-delimited or Excel formats. Each type of report mentioned can be qualified by a specific time period, i.e., today, last seven days, month to date, last 30 days, year to date, last 12 months, or a custom time frame, and can be filtered by specified IP address ranges if desired. The "Session Report" type can be used to generate reports on the total number of sessions conducted with data on the average session length, total number of pages viewed, and average number of pages viewed per session. The "Search Report" feature can be used to analyze both the total number of keyword and subject searches, the top 10 keywords and subjects input by users, as well as the total number of searches completed. "LinkOut Reports" show the number of times that users have clicked on links by various categories–individual journal titles, aggregator, aggregator and resource, publisher, and vendor–for any of the time periods mentioned above.

LINKSOURCE

As mentioned earlier, LinkSource is EBSCO's OpenURL-compliant link resolver software that facilitates centralized access to the library's Web-based resources no matter where they reside. Users can start a search with any database service that the library provides that has been profiled in LinkSource and be connected to subscribed resources on other platforms. Figure 4 shows how

FIGURE 4. LinkSource Generated Icon and Text for Additional Access Options

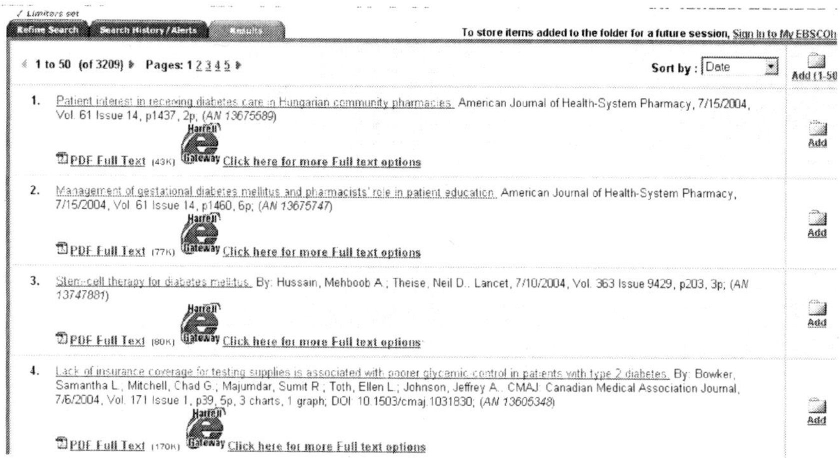

the link to other options can appear in a database search. A library can edit both the icon and the text message that is used.

For libraries that purchase the A-to-Z service, the same data file that was prepared for the A-to-Z implementation can be used in the implementation of LinkSource. In addition, the library must notify their database providers that the library is a LinkSource subscriber in order to have the appropriate URL connections established. Information about the links to be sent to vendors is posted on the EBSCO support site.

When all of the settings are completed, a citation that is found through a search in OVID, or Web of Knowledge, or ProQuest, for example, will show a link that leads the user to various options for acquiring the document. A menu of all of the access options for a citation is created based on policies configured by the library. For non-full-text items, users can be directed to the library catalog, to a serials list, to an interlibrary loan request form, or to a commercial document delivery order form. For citations with full-text access, those links are listed as well.

LinkSource in itself is not a database or search interface, but instead is a gateway that streamlines the steps that users must take to reach a needed document. Another option that is available is that a user can enter a known citation directly into LinkSource using a "submit" menu to locate a source for an article without having to first search for content in a database. Usage statistics can also be generated from LinkSource to track content access from all targets and sources, which would be helpful with collection development and in assessing the level of use of the library's databases.

CONCLUSION

After the purchase of the A-to-Z and LinkSource products in May 2004, the Harrell Library staff began the implementation process by reading the extensive documentation, both print and online, that was available from EBSCO about the different features of the software. A two-day training session with an EBSCO technical staff member was held the first week of June 2004. The next phase included the selection of title packages through the Title Maintenance Wizard to create a master list for downloading and editing. Testing was done to see how edits would appear on the A-to-Z list and to determine what features would be included in the list displayed to the public. The review and editing of the master list–comparing it with the library's existing Web list, making additions and corrections, resolving problems with proxy addresses, and adding special notes to the master list–took approximately three months to complete with the full-time equivalent of one staff person. Over 15,000 lines of data were reviewed and edited. The assistance of the technical staff member from EBSCO was invaluable with the conversion of data from the library's existing Web site, the programming to remove proxy access from freely accessible titles, and for supplying the information to set up profiles between LinkSource and various database suppliers used by the library.

One difference with the new A-to-Z list from the library's former title list that will take some time for users to become familiar with is the different alphabetization that is used between the lists. The former title list was alphabetized by significant words ignoring articles between words. The EBSCO A-to-Z product follows the strict alphabetical order of every word including articles unless the data line would be edited otherwise. This editing, however, would make the title a "custom title" that requires maintenance by the library. Suggestions for improvement to the A-to-Z product include: being able to edit data directly online without having to upload/download a spreadsheet; allow that cosmetic edits would not change the title status to a "custom title"; have the option to ignore articles in the alphabetization of the list; and include MeSH or Medical Subject Headings or other subject taxonomies in place of the Library of Congress hierarchy for the subject index.

The Harrell Library looks forward to continued use of the A-to-Z and LinkSource products with the hope that links to journals will be better maintained, that any changes initiated from publishers will be kept more up to date with the use of the EBSCO services, that users will be kept more aware of the resources that are available no matter what search interface they prefer to use, and that collection development will be enhanced with more complete statistics on the use of full-text electronic resources.

Evolutionary Approach
to Managing E-Resources

Richard P. Jasper
Laura Sheble

SUMMARY. Over the past five years the Wayne State University Library System has become a national leader in the transition from print to electronic, with nearly 60% of the $7 million annual materials budget going to pay for electronic resources. Learning how to manage these resources has been an evolutionary process. This article discusses the WSULS experience with regards to: (1) the transition from print to electronic, (2) the current state of e-resources management, and (3) future directions in utilizing staff and technology to address e-resource issues. *[Article copies available for a fee from The Haworth Document Delivery Service: 1-800-HAWORTH. E-mail address: <docdelivery@haworthpress.com>*

Richard P. Jasper (MLn, Emory University, 1985) is Director of Resource Services, Wayne State University Library System, 5150 Anthony Wayne Drive, Detroit, MI 48202.

Laura Sheble (MLIS, Wayne State University, 2002) is Electronic Resources Librarian, Wayne State University Library System, 5150 Anthony Wayne Drive, Detroit, MI 48202.

The authors would like to express their appreciation to the following staff at Wayne State University for their contributions to this article: Stephen D. Corrsin, Head of Acquisitions; Frances M. Krempasky, Head of Cataloging; Diane N. Paldan, Serials/Preservation Librarian; Jeffrey G. Trzeciak, Director, Library Computing and Media Services; Georgia A. Clark, Director, Arthur Neef Law Library; Shawn McCann, Web Librarian; and Matthew Decker, Library Webmaster.

[Haworth co-indexing entry note]: "Evolutionary Approach to Managing E-Resources." Jasper, Richard P. and Laura Sheble. Co-published simultaneously in *The Serials Librarian* (The Haworth Information Press, an imprint of The Haworth Press, Inc.) Vol. 47, No. 4, 2005, pp. 55-70; and: *Electronic Journal Management Systems: Experiences from the Field* (ed: Gary Ives) The Haworth Information Press, an imprint of The Haworth Press, Inc., 2005, pp. 55-70. Single or multiple copies of this article are available for a fee from The Haworth Document Delivery Service [1-800-HAWORTH, 9:00 a.m. - 5:00 p.m. (EST). E-mail address: docdelivery@haworthpress.com].

Digital Object Identifier: 10.1300/J123v47n04_07

KEYWORDS. Electronic resources, online journals, SFX, Serials Solutions

INTRODUCTION

Over the past five years the Wayne State University Library System has dramatically changed the manner in which it presents journal literature to its students, faculty, and staff. In that time we have moved from a system that was overwhelmingly reliant on print to one in which the primary form of access is electronic.

The Association of Research Libraries' (2003) report on libraries' expenditures for electronic resources shows that during 2001-2002 the percentage of Wayne State's materials budget devoted to online was 44.96%. In that report Wayne State was tied in that category with the University of Montreal and exceeded only by the University of Cincinnati (44.97%.) Since that time the proportion of over materials budget devoted to electronic resources has continued to increase, with approximately 60% of the acquisitions budget for Fiscal Year 2003-2004 devoted to online materials Likewise, at this point nearly two-thirds of our 18,000 periodical titles are available in electronic format and nearly half of those are available only in electronic format.

During this time our approach to managing e-resources has continued to evolve and change. There has been a steady progression in the number and variety of tools we use to make these highly prized resources available to our patrons. There have been changes in staffing, as well, and those changes are beginning to accelerate. We are, in fact, on the cusp on being able to hand off a significant portion of the responsibility for day-to-day management of e-resource issues from high level (and highly paid) librarian staff to our talented albeit more focused support staff.

In many ways, the rate and nature of change Wayne State has experienced over the past five years makes us a typical North American research library. If anything sets us apart, it is the degree to which we have embraced these changes, devoting materials expenditures, technology, and staffing to the task of completing the move from print to electronic. We think our experience at Wayne has been illustrative and consequently in this article we will describe:

- The arc of Wayne State's move from print to electronic
- The current state of e-resources management at Wayne State, including:
  - The role of the Library Website as principal point of entry for accessing Wayne's e-resources

- The opportunities and challenges existing in this current state
- Our experience with Serials Solutions and SFX (and why we continue to maintain both)
    - New positions and staffing strategies employed to make all this work
- Where we think we are headed, in terms of
    - additional tools
    - changing roles for existing staff

THE MOVE FROM PRINT TO ELECTRONIC: HOW DID WE GET HERE?

Although Wayne State made electronic resources (in the form of CD-ROMs and other online databases) available to its users from fairly early on, its entrée into the world of online journals was somewhat belated.

The first systemwide Web page for the Wayne State libraries debuted sometime in 1997. It included an e-resources page and subject guides. Concurrently, Wayne staff members were becoming aware through a variety of means that electronic resources were available for us to use. Links to these resources were activated; if represented anywhere in the library system they appeared in Web-based subject guides but there was no systematic attempt to make a listing of all e-resources available in a single place. Meantime, Cataloging staff as early as 1998 were experimenting with creating records for online journals in Wayne's integrated library system.

The Library System made another great leap forward in 1998 by agreeing to take part in the Michigan Library Consortium's licensing of the Academic Press IDEAL e-journal platform, electing to provide only e-access to many important titles that had previously been available electronically.

Confronted with the need to deal systematically with a large group of e-journal titles, the Library System in late 1998/early 1999 appointed the Electronic Resources Integration Task Force, a cross-sectional working group consisting of technical services librarians, systems staff, and collection managers, to develop recommendations regarding how the libraries should handle electronic resources.

By December 1999 ERITF had completed its work. The ensuing report to what was then known as the Library Management Group addressed several e-resource issues, including:

- prioritization of cataloging tasks
- communication between Selectors and Cataloging
- single versus separate record cataloging

ERITF (1999) recommended that priorities for cataloging work be established collaboratively between Cataloging and Selectors, and that Selector

Teams establish point persons to coordinate prioritization and to serve as a point of contact for cataloging questions, especially those concerning priorities and maintenance. It was decided that cataloging new resources was a higher priority than retrospective cataloging, and cataloging paid resources a higher priority than 'free.' It was recommended that Websites should receive separate record cataloging on a selective or case-by-case basis, and that link checker technologies be investigated. Most importantly, ERITF recommended the use of single hybrid records as much as possible; though it was noted separate records would likely be used if records were purchased for package of e-resource titles.

The Library System proceeded to implement the ERITF recommendations but quickly found that the number and variety of e-resources becoming available far outstripped the capacity of Cataloging staff to keep up. With that in mind the Library System in 2001 turned to Serials Solutions as a means of rapidly making available links to the burgeoning number of e-resources.

Later that year the advent of a new dean resulted in the formulation of a new set of strategic directions for the Library System, one of which emphasized the need to transition library resources from print to electronic. By the end of 2001 the Library System had completed an agreement with Elsevier for its ScienceDirect product, eliminating virtually all of Wayne's print Elsevier subscriptions in favor of being able to provide access to Elsevier's entire online corpus.

Additional reorganization efforts at Wayne in 2002 identified a number of staffing issues that needed to be resolved in order to facilitate the transition to a primarily electronic environment, including:

- the need for a systemwide collection management officer to address e-resource issues
- the need for a full-time Web librarian to address networking connectivity issues
- the need for a full-time electronic resources librarian to address problems related to access and electronic content

All three positions were filled during 2003, with many thanks due to the University Administration, which proved supportive of the Library System's reorganization efforts despite the serious budget crunch facing the State of Michigan.

Concurrent with the filling of these positions, Wayne State embarked on two additional technological upgrades to help facilitate ease of access to electronic resources, implementing:

- EZProxy software to allow authorized patrons to easily access e-resources from off campus,
- SFX link-resolver technology

All of these developments bring us to our current state, one in which the large majority of our journal titles are available electronically as well as in print (or only electronically) and in which 60% or more of our annual materials budget goes to pay for electronic resources. The following section discusses the ways in which these developments are currently being played out and the opportunities and challenges each has presented.

CURRENT STATE

At this point Wayne State relies on a number of different tools, both technological and organizational, to manage electronic resources. In terms of tools, the Library Website, the OPAC, Serials Solutions, and SFX all play a role in providing access to electronic resources. In terms of staffing, an ad hoc working group of technical services librarians has evolved to include collection managers and two new positions (electronic resources librarian and Web librarian); together these staff members comprise the "first responders" to any problem involving access to electronic resources. The way in which we have deployed technological and organizational tools to deal with e-resources is the subject of this section.

The Library Website as Principal Point of Entry

http://www.lib.wayne.edu

At present the Library Website connects users to electronic resources through four paths:

- Links to the OPAC
- Database link pages
- Subject Guides, created with *ResearchGuide* software, an open source software package
- Online Journals page, which consists of the E-Journal Finder search and browse interfaces to Serials Solutions and the SFX Citation Linker

OPAC

http://webpac.wayne.edu/webpac-bin/wgbroker?new+-access+top.wsu

The library catalog plays a central though not a solitary role in providing access to electronic resources. Not only are electronic resources cataloged, but the library catalog also mediates access to electronic resources from the Library Website. From the Website, links to electronic resources on the Database pages and Subject Guides link first to a record in the Library catalog, and then, through the record, to the resource itself.

By 2002, the 2000 ERITF recommendations (described above) were largely in place, and absorbed into the workflow. Database Management had implemented link checking and correction or URL address in bibliographic records, including government documents. With greater experience of the e-resource world, it also became clear that exceptions would remain the rule in the electronic environment for a considerable length of time, that publishers and vendors would continue to provide online resources, but in many different formats and systems, and that underlying standards development would not be a feature of the near future. Therefore, in order to provide the most consistent e-resource information in the cataloging, Cataloging extended the ERITF guidelines to include the following practices.

1. Full title-by-title cataloging would be the rule whenever possible, whether the title is part of a larger database, or an individual title. This may include record selection, merging of electronic and print title formats, and collapsing of multiple electronic format records in order to adhere to the single hybrid record recommendation developed by ERITF.
2. Full cataloging would also be performed at the aggregator database level.
3. Cataloging will decide whether to purchase individual title records for large databases on a vendor or database-specific basis. A system for loading records into the catalog was developed between Systems and Cataloging. Typically, these records are not combined with other records of the same title, thus breaking with the single record recommendation because of the need to remove them as titles are added, removed, and discontinued in aggregator databases, and when resource licenses significantly change or are not renewed.
4. On special request, Cataloging will also:
    a. Add links to a search page of a database containing a title to the record for that title when it was not possible to link to the resource at the title level, with notes explaining access.
    b. Add titles of individual (constituent) works in a database to 740 fields in the database record.
    c. Link records of individual titles that are part of a larger package through aggregate titles in the 773 field.
    d. Create provisional bibliographic records in the online catalog (e.g., Elephant Research Foundation Bibliography Website).

Moving forward, Cataloging is reviewing opportunities to purchase records from a vendor and working on Data Normalization/Standardization projects. We are keenly aware that at this point managing our e-resources means maintaining disparate information in multiple databases.

Database Links Pages

http://www.lib.wayne.edu/resources/articles_databases/index.php

The Frequently Used Databases (FUD) page was the first of database links pages, designed to serve as a jump page or quick links list for frequently used databases. In a draft recommendation in 2000, the Electronic Resources Integration Task Force (ERITF) suggested that resources be Selected for inclusion on this page based on fund type and recommendation by Selector teams: Resources purchased on the electronic pool fund, which covers purchases, would be given first consideration, along with up to 10 other resources recommended by each of the three selector teams (Social Sciences [includes Law], Humanities/Fine Arts and Science/Technology/Medicine). Changes to the page were to be submitted by Selector teams rather than individual librarians.

The FUD page consists of titles of selected resources and links to the catalog record for the resource. Resource descriptions are not directly included on the FUD page. Instead, links on the FUD page connect to the bibliographic display in the OPAC for a given resource.

In addition to the Frequently Used Databases page, a complete alphabetical list of databases was created. While the FUD page continued to be a static links page, the Full Alphabetic List is created dynamically based on bibliographic records. The list is generated based on location codes in the 856 field and includes a description of the resource pulled from the 520 field, and refreshed weekly. By generating database lists based on catalog records, not only was the need to separately update the Web pages eliminated, but also enabled us to treat updates to the lists as catalog updates, present select information uniformly through multiple interfaces, and merge maintenance tasks into current workflows. Subsequently, Undergraduate, Graduate, Law, Medicine, and Science and Engineering database pages were added, created on the model of the Full Alphabetic List. Currently, tabs visually link and are used to navigate between database pages.

Subject Guides

http://www.lib.wayne.edu/resources/subject_guides/index.php

Library Website subject guides are created and maintained by librarian subject area specialists, also known as *Selectors*. Generally, a Selector acts as liaison to a University department and is also responsible for creating and maintaining a *Subject Resource and Guide* Web page for the department. Selectors are encouraged to include resources in all formats in the guides, focusing on those tools that are appropriate to the subject area and primary user groups. Subject guides for the Schools of Law and Medicine in many cases are handled and managed differently than those of other University departments.

Before the redesign of the library Website in 2002, subject guides were created through manual and DreamWeaver-facilitated HTML coding. As a result, the subject guides differed markedly from each other, at least in part due to varying levels of comfort and interest in Web development among Selectors. Not only was there a lack of consistency in the presentation of resources but also in the number and variety of subject guides, with many subject disciplines unrepresented. During 2003 the library systems group implemented *Research Guide*, a PHP and MySQL-based open source package for creating and maintaining subject guides. Though use of this software was initially optional, the consistent ability to offer a consistent look and feel to subject guides and to centrally manage navigation between subject guides, Selector contact information, and other aspects of the Website soon led to mandatory adoption of the software by Selectors.

Selectors present electronic resources in the subject guides to varying degrees, depending on the resources available in the subject area, the familiarity of a Selector with electronic resources, and the needs expressed by user groups in the corresponding department. Electronic resources of all types (including subscribed and freely available journals, databases, e-books, and Internet sites) are included in subject guides. Selectors are strongly encouraged to provide links to OPAC displays corresponding to each resource, regardless of resource type or format. Users may connect to online resources from URLs included in the records.

Online Journals Page

http://www.lib.wayne.edu/resources/journals/index.php

The last of the main paths to online resources, the Online Journals page facilitates access to full-text online journals via two resources: a link to the SFX citation linker and the Serials Solutions serials management package.

The Online Journals page evolved from what was once called the Alphabetic List of Journals and the E-Journal Finder. Under these earlier iterations, this resource consisted of an alphabetical listing of full-text journals presented in multiple HTML-encoded reports that the Library System received from Serials Solutions on a monthly basis. Library staff would check changes and updates to the reports when they arrived and then upload the new reports to the server, replacing the older outdated reports.

More recently, with the implementation of Serials Solutions' *E-Journal Portal*, Wayne State locally hosts a single Web page, the Online Journals page, from which users may initiate title and ISSN searches and alphabetical and subject browses. Once a search or browse is initiated from this page, the user is then interacting with the Serials Solutions database, hosted on Serials Solutions servers but with an interface customized for Wayne State University Libraries. Wayne State's use of SFX and Serials Solutions is discussed more in depth separately.

Opportunities and Challenges

The Library Website as a medium to connect users to electronic resources has presented a number of unique opportunities and challenges. On the one hand, Web technologies enable the Library System to facilitate access to a variety of resources in a visually compact format in both general and focused subject areas and by resource type. According to Website statistics, Web pages that facilitate access to electronic resources, and the Frequently Used Databases and Online Journals page in particular, are popular with library users. Public services librarians report that undergraduates and users new to a given subject area find the library Website useful as a mechanism for resource discovery. More experienced library users who perform in-depth research in a particular subject area are more likely to use portions of the Website as jump pages to resources they use frequently.

Outside of structural questions, content management and maintenance has been the main challenge facing the Library System in effectively using the library Website as a means to connect users to electronic resources. While additions, deletions, and changes to electronic resource records in the library catalog are a challenge to track and keep up with, they are reported and processed in a standard codified workflow that is an extension of the workflow traditionally followed for resources in other formats.

In contrast, workflows for updates to the library Website resources have not been as strictly codified, especially between service groups. Additionally, while a change to a catalog record for any given resource can be initiated by a single staff member, or even a patron, it was initially stated that before a change to a database link page could be submitted, it was first necessary to develop a consensus within a selector team, and then to submit a request for the change as a team.

Some see the lack of guidelines regarding the use and purpose of the Subject Guides versus the Database listings an obstacle as well. Other complications arise from the nature of a basically static Internet display. While the library catalog can essentially hold information for an infinite number of resources, there is a limit to the number of elements that can be presented in a given Web page and a limit to the number of resources and the number of different paths to resources that can effectively be presented and maintained in an environment of dispersed content management. We anticipate that some of these challenges will be overcome with migration to an ILS that will enable us to more closely integrate the catalog with the Library Website through the use of additional functionalities such as subject scoping.

Serials Solutions and SFX

As discussed previously, library patron interaction with the Serials Solutions database begins at the Online Journals page. The Serials Solutions serials management package was adopted at Wayne State for four main reasons:

- To facilitate access to online journals by title through a format specific browsable user interface
- To augment access to online journal content effectively hidden in provider databases due to the lack of title-level links
- To facilitate tracking of database content as titles drop out of or are added to provider databases.
- To facilitate quicker access to new electronic resources. In 2001, when Serials Solutions was implemented, the rate at which electronic resources were being added to the collection was far greater than what could be processed in cataloging due to staffing constraints.

Serials Solutions is outgrowing earlier evaluations and observations made by Sitko et al. (2002) and Duranceau (2002). While the simplicity of the Serials Solutions serials management product may have once been both its greatest strength and greatest limitation, the current Serials Solution serials management suite of products is able to offer a greater range of services, based on the amount of time library staff is able to invest in data customization, and the services to which the library subscribes. Currently, Wayne State subscribes only to the serials management services available through Serials Solutions, including the E-Journal Portal. Both the staff and user side interfaces continue the tradition of simplicity of use present in earlier versions of the product. Through the Serials Solutions staff side interface, library staff members select resources at the package level; often a database, but sometimes at a finer level of granularity within a provider site, for instance, at the publisher level in a multi-publisher database or Website. If applicable, a staff member selects specific titles within a given resource that the library licenses and then specifies custom URLs to access the resource.

Two major benefits of the simplicity of this resource have been our abilities (1) to invest a minimal amount of valuable staff time in the maintenance of the database and (2) to assign specific database update tasks to frontline staff. The greatest drawback to the information presented to the public was that–and this is stated explicitly on the Website–*the holdings information presented for a given title represent what is made available online by the provider of that resource and may not be an accurate reflection of the holdings of the Wayne State University collection*.

In early 2004, it became possible to customize library holdings in Serials Solutions, with both ordinate and relative date specifications (e.g., "from 1997 to . . ." or "from last year's volume to this year's volume . . ."). While Serials Solutions has maintained an intuitive, user-friendly interface, entry of library-specific holdings information is a time-consuming activity and one to which we have allocated staff resources only for heavily used and problematic titles and packages. Whether we will be able to allocate further resources to holdings customization in the future remains unclear.

In addition to holdings customization, the Serials Solutions package has been augmented with several other useful features in late 2003 and 2004. For example, with the implementation of the *E-Journal Portal* feature, updates we make to our data are available to users within 24 hours; previously this information did not display to users until after we had uploaded new HTML reports at the end of the month. Likewise, in place of the HTML reports we now receive reports in spreadsheet-friendly formats. We were able to use URL and title lists from these reports to include in our catalog; the alternative would have been to generate URLs on a title-by-title basis from the provider's Website. We have also begun to explore using the Overlap Analysis feature for collection development purposes and are testing the use of links to various levels of granularity within the Subject browse functionality of the public interface in our Subject Guides.

Because we are passively dependant on the ability of any third party resource to give us accurate holdings information for resources that have revolving content doors, we can only assume that our ability to provide more accurate access to online holdings has been enhanced at least somewhat by the adoption of this or any resource. Until we are able to implement a comprehensive tracking process for databases that have a revolving content door, we begrudgingly admit that it is inevitable that we will not be able to maintain accurate holdings for all resources.

The work we do with Serials Solutions (implemented in 2001) occurs in tandem with our work in SFX and is often performed by the staff members. Implementation of SFX began with training in the spring of 2003, and has progressed to date. Previous experimentation with an open source link resolver software package proved that while the functionality of the open source package was generally satisfactory, database maintenance and other issues would require more staff hours than available. Then, in 2003, Wayne State had the opportunity to join in a consortial purchase of ExLibris' SFX. A market and needs analysis indicated that SFX was compatible with the primary needs of Wayne State from a link resolver package.

Implementation began with packages believed to give the greatest return for time invested. Packages were evaluated in terms of ease of implementation and the number and use of resources within the packages. Selector teams contributed to the activation process first by prioritizing resources to be activated in their subject area, and second by becoming involved in testing and reviewing activated packages. This was a combination of formal and informal processes. As of August 2004, approximately 3/4 of Wayne State's OpenURL-compatible electronic resources have been activated. Along with the activation of source and target resources, we've also activated select SFX services, including the Citation Linker and OpenURL Generator. Activation of the remaining 1/4 of WSU resources is expected to progress less rapidly than the first 3/4 despite our increased knowledge of the product since these resources generally require more detailed treatment or configuration.

New Positions and Staffing Strategies

Prior to 2003–and despite momentous changes in the scale and variety of its e-resource offerings–the Library System had no individual staff member whose position was principally (much less solely) devoted to e-resources management. The Strategic Planning Report that served as the foundation for an across the board reorganization of the Library System in 2002 specified as urgent needs the hiring of both an electronic resources librarian (to be located in Resource Services, Wayne's combined collection management and technical services organization) and a Web librarian (to work in Library Computing and Media Services.)

As observed by Jasper (2002), one approach to dealing with e-resource issues when staff specifically dedicated to these activities are unavailable is to rely on collaboration among front-line librarians to address e-resource issues when funding for staff specifically dedicated to these activities has been unavailable. This approach is still employed at Wayne State even though we now also have an electronic resources librarian and a Web librarian to focus on user complaints and accessibility issues.

Historically, this group consisted of representatives of traditional technical services functional areas, including cataloging, acquisitions, database management, and serials. All members of the informal group were subscribed to *AskTS*, an online distribution list that served (and still serves) as a complaint/concern repository for library staff regarding technical service operations, including the management of e-resources. As our experience with electronic resources evolved (and as the Library System was reorganized), additional staff were added to the group, including the Library System's two collection management coordinators, the Director of Resource Services, and then (both hired in 2003) the Library System's first electronic resources librarian and its first Web librarian.

Current library practices encourages library staff to submit issues directly to the *AskTS* Listserv for resolution by the first responders. These issues are generally presented by Information Services staff that mediate questions from library users through their roles in providing reference, instruction, and liaison services. The use of this basic technology has provided a flexible and inclusive means through which it has been possible to effectively troubleshoot issues as they arise. The shared communication environment has also provided a forum for discussing issues as they arise and has served as a mechanism by which staff working in different functional areas can share expertise and learn from each other's experiences.

Two drawbacks to this approach have been the reliance on specific staff members who are decision makers in relation to electronic resources, without a standard way of including backups for these individuals when they are not available, and the lack of a centralized issue tracking system. The first of these issues may be addressed at an organizational level and the second may be addressed with a system designed to supplement triage and tracking procedures.

THE FUTURE: WHERE ARE WE GOING NEXT?

In the coming year we expect to see additional significant changes in the areas of technology and staffing, specifically:

1. We will be implementing the *Electronic Resources Manager* component of III's Millennium integrated library system.
2. We will redesign technical services workflow to (among other things) allow front-line support staff to take on many of the routine tasks associated with e-resources management.

Our aspirations for each of these areas are discussed in this section.

Preparing for the ERM

We are currently implementing the Millennium integrated library system of Innovative Interfaces Inc. (III). Implementation of the Electronic Resources Manager (ERM) module of Millennium is expected to begin in fall 2004. While we don't expect the ERM to be the silver bullet any more than SFX, Serials Solutions, the Library Website, or the catalog have been, we do expect to gain a number of distinct advantages over our current environment. We see the ERM as a place to centralize a good deal of the administrative information associated with our electronic resources.

Resource Services staff have begun to prepare for ERM implementation with several smaller projects, that, though overlapping, generally fall into three categories: (1) collocation of information, (2) license analysis, and (3) system capabilities. Due to organizational changes with restructuring that occurred in 2002-03 and traditional divisions of responsibilities, we've found that some information, such as administrative information, and to a lesser degree, vendor contact information, has been dispersed throughout the Library System. Since the ERM will enable us to centrally manage or track this information, we've increased our efforts to gather this information and have begun talks to further delineate responsibilities in relation to resource management. A second major project has been the focus on electronic resource license agreements. Acquisitions has analyzed license agreements according to parameters that we believe will be helpful to library staff use and presentation of resources and according to what we believe we will be able to accommodate in ERM. Additionally, we have begun scanning our current license agreements to pdf files. These files will be made available to library staff on a password-authenticated basis, through *DocuTrek*, our electronic reserves system. We plan to link to electronic copies of license agreements through the ERM once this functionality is implemented.

Once ERM is implemented, we believe we will be able to manage electronic resource information more effectively and more efficiently. We expect that it will be easier to connect problems with specific e-journal titles with background–publisher, aggregator, consortium, licensing and subscription–information. We also expect that the availability of a central repository for information previously dispersed throughout the system will effectively serve as an institutional memory that may help mitigate the effects of staff turnover and changes in responsibilities. Fortunate or not, though we may be down a spreadsheet or two, we will retain and continue to rely on our arsenal of information sources and resources for electronic resource information, including our subscription agent's database, the serials management packages, platform and publisher resources and databases, and the more traditional ILS modules.

Implications for Reorganizing and Reassigning Staff

Heretofore the challenges associated with acquiring, paying for, setting up, and maintaining access to individual e-journal titles have required a set of complex problem-solving skills that more typically resides with librarians than with support staff. Over the years we have learned by doing and part of what we have learned is that a significant number of tasks associated with managing e-resources are in fact fairly straightforward. Likewise, as e-resources have proliferated, the number of times these straightforward tasks need to be performed in quantity has likewise expanded.

A good example of this is the work we do when managing the transition of an individual publisher's titles from print to electronic. As members of the Michigan Library Consortium, Wayne State has agreed to participate in a number of consortial purchases for various publishers' online journal packages. In each case, we have to determine:

- How many are currently held by our library?
- How many have traditionally been held?
- How many of the titles not held by Wayne State are held by other libraries in the consortium?
- Are we already providing e-access to some or all of these titles through some other means?

At present there is no automated way of determining the answers to these questions, largely because of the way our records have been structured but partly because of the historical nuances associated with our subscriptions. This type of research is usually fairly straightforward but given the number of titles (often hundreds for an individual publisher) it can be extremely time-consuming. Having our e-resources librarian spend time on this work would have a negative impact on her ability to deal directly with end-users on accessibility issues. On the other hand, a support staff member who in times past would have spent almost all of her time on checking in print journal issues could likewise research, record, synopsize, and present this information, and do so without backlogging end-user requests.

Likewise, with SFX we devoted a significant amount of high level staff time for the better part of six months to get the software, procedures, and content set up and running. Now that most of the research and investigation needed to activate various sources and targets has been completed we are at a point where we can begin seriously looking at the possibility of having additions to content handled by support staff.

In the coming year our goal is to examine all technical services workflow with an eye toward shifting the focus of our work so that–as with the materials budget–the majority of our staff time is spent dealing with electronic resources.

CONCLUSION

Over the past five years the Wayne State University Library System has experienced a fundamental change in its approach to providing resources for its patrons, shifting from a predominantly print environment to one in which electronic resources are given first priority. This shift has been accompanied by significant changes in library funding (electronic resources now comprise 60% of the library materials budget), form of access (the library Website is now the principal means for approaching the collection, with the library catalog one of several tools co-located within the Website), and staffing (addition of the electronic resources librarian and Web librarian, pending changes in responsibility for support staff).

These changes have been evolutionary in nature. Just as electronic publishing is evolving, so too is our understanding of what it takes to manage electronic resources effectively. Five years ago we could not have predicted where exactly this journey would take us. Along the way we have learned that no single tool (the library catalog, the library Website, Serials Solutions, SFX) and no single strategy (collaborative teams, individual staff devoted full-time to electronic resources) has been "the answer." Instead each new tool and each new strategy has allowed us to do new things, to address many (but not all) of our concerns regarding electronic resources, and prompted us to keep looking and keep thinking.

We have learned enough, in other words, to have some fairly clear ideas regarding how much of the work associated with managing electronic resources (everything from licensing and set up to resolving e-access problems and doing background research in support of possible changes in content offerings) needs to be done at a fairly high level of staffing, how much of it could legitimately be handed off to library support staff. Our challenge in the coming year is to ensure that this latest transition occurs in a way that maximizes the abilities of existing library staff and therefore the effectiveness of the Library System in managing e-resources.

REFERENCES

Association for Research Libraries. (2003) *ARL Supplementary Statistics for 2001-2002*, 14-16.

Duranceau, E.F. (2002). Electronic journal forum: E-journal package-content tracking services, *Serials Review*, 28(1): 49-52.

Electronic Resources Integration Task Force (ERITF). Wayne State University Library System. (1999) *Recommendations for Providing and Managing Remote Access Electronic Publications*, 1-4.

Jasper, R.P. Collaborative roles in managing electronic publications [At the Houston Academy of Medicine-Texas Medical Center]. *Library Collections, Acquisitions, and Technical Services* v. 26 no 4 (Winter 2002) pp. 355-61.

Sitko, M., Tafuri, N., Szcxyrbak, G., & Park, T. (2002). E-journal management systems: Trends, trials, and trade-offs, *Serials Review*, 28(3): 176-194.

Transition to E-Journals
at Texas A&M University, 1995-2004

Gary Ives

SUMMARY. From the first record of a Web-based electronic journal at Texas A&M in 1995, to a collection of over 35,000 unique electronic titles today, electronic delivery of journal content has shifted from the exotic to the expected mode of delivery in less than 10 years. In the last 3 years, we have moved aggressively to electronic-only licensing from publishers which assure permanent access rights, with more than 3,000 of over 9,000 publisher subscriptions now received electronic only. This paper describes the growth of our electronic collections, the evolution of our Web site as a listing and finding tool, and the transitions of managing electronic collections first manually, then with Serials Solutions, and now with SFX. *[Article copies available for a fee from The Haworth Document Delivery Service: 1-800-HAWORTH. E-mail address: <docdelivery@haworthpress.com> Website: <http://www.HaworthPress.com> © 2005 by The Haworth Press, Inc. All rights reserved.]*

KEYWORDS. Electronic journal management systems, SFX, Serials Solutions, link resolver, Texas A&M University

Gary Ives is Assistant Director of Acquisitions and Coordinator of Electronic Resources, Texas A&M University Libraries, 5000 TAMU, College Station, TX 77843-5000 (E-mail: gives@lib-gw.tamu.edu).

[Haworth co-indexing entry note]: "Transition to E-Journals at Texas A&M University, 1995-2004." Ives, Gary. Co-published simultaneously in *The Serials Librarian* (The Haworth Information Press, an imprint of The Haworth Press, Inc.) Vol. 47, No. 4, 2005, pp. 71-78; and: *Electronic Journal Management Systems: Experiences from the Field* (ed: Gary Ives) The Haworth Information Press, an imprint of The Haworth Press, Inc., 2005, pp. 71-78. Single or multiple copies of this article are available for a fee from The Haworth Document Delivery Service [1-800-HAWORTH, 9:00 a.m. - 5:00 p.m. (EST). E-mail address: docdelivery@haworthpress.com].

Digital Object Identifier: 10.1300/J123v47n04_08

Texas A&M University Libraries serve over 40,000 faculty, staff, and student FTEs, including the researchers and staff of 7 agencies and extension services which have the College Station campus as their home. In FY 2002-2003, the Libraries ranked 6th among all ARL libraries in expenditures for electronic resources, and in FY 2004-2005, the Libraries' total materials budget will exceed 10 million dollars for the first time. As of fall 2004, the Libraries' catalogs and Web site offer over 60,000 electronic resources, including more than 35,000 unique serial titles. And the totals continue to grow.

I trace the beginning of our electronic journal collections at Texas A&M University to an announcement in our April 1995 Medical Sciences Library Newsletter for the new title *Emerging Infectious Diseases* (http://www.cdc.gov/ncidod/EID/index.htm). This journal was born digitally in January 1995, published by the Centers for Disease Control and Prevention, Atlanta, and is now in its 10th year. The very next month, May 1995, the Medical Sciences Library's Web site was launched. This site provided an HTML browse list of biomedicine and veterinary medicine electronic journal titles from 1995 until it was retired in early 2003 (see Figure 1).

FIGURE 1. Medical Sciences Library Electronic Journals List, Early 2003

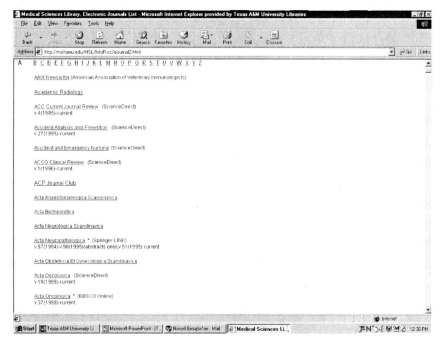

From this beginning in 1995, the Medical Sciences Library saw its electronic journal collection grow, at first modestly, but then explosively: 21 titles by the end of 1997; 280 by the end of 1998; 685 by the end of 1999; over 1,400 by the end of 2001; and over 2,200 titles by the time the Web list was retired in early 2003.

In the broader context of the entire Texas A&M University campus, the growth of electronic journals has been even more dramatic. From 1998 to early 2003, Evans Library maintained a Web site which included what was called a Public Access Menu, or PAM (see Figure 2). Through this interface, a user could browse an alphabetized list of titles by selecting a letter. Or the user could do a simple keyword search on the title or publisher. The example shown in Figure 2 is a keyword search on the word "colloid."

Figure 3 shows the search results as a list of links for titles containing the word "colloid." The Public Access Menu searched a SQL database, which was maintained manually. By 1998, we had over 1,100 titles listed in the database; by 1999 we had over 1,700 titles listed; by 2001, we listed over 3,000 titles. And by the fall of 2002, just prior to our implementation of Serials Solutions, we listed over 4,200 titles.

The story of our experience with electronic journals follows the same script as most other academic libraries. The explosion in the availability of electronic

FIGURE 2. Evans Library Public Access Menu (PAM), Early 2003

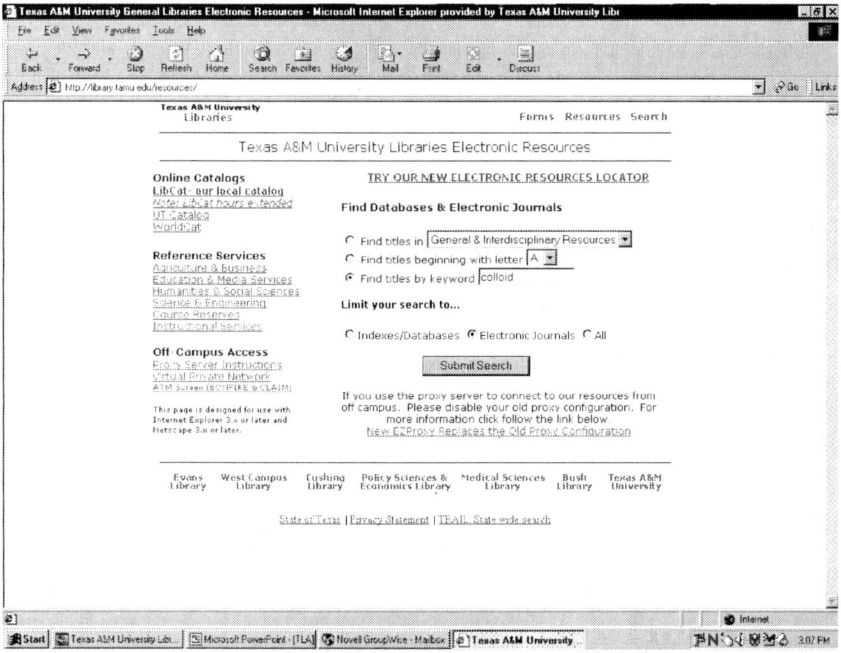

FIGURE 3. Public Access Menu Search Results for "Colloid"

titles, the dynamic nature of availability and access, and the "overnight" popularity of electronic access have challenged our ability to deliver services and content at the level our users are demanding. Manual systems proved inadequate in keeping up with the workload. By the summer of 2002, we were convinced at both at the Medical Sciences Library and the Evans Library that we needed a content tracking service. After reviewing the services then available, we selected Serials Solutions under pricing made available through Amigos Library Services.

Our service from Serials Solutions consisted of a bimonthly datafeed of our subscribed titles from publishers and aggregators. In one batch load to our existing SQL database, the first datafeed we received in the fall of 2002 accomplished (at least) 3 things for us:

- We had recently signed a license for the 700+ Kluwer journal titles, but they were not represented in either our catalog or Web site. What earlier would have taken weeks or months to compile and enter into the SQL database was done overnight.
- Likewise, dozens of titles from numerous publishers (constituting our "backlog") were activated in Serials Solutions and were part of our initial load.

- Finally, we had never had the means to include on our Web site (let alone our catalog) titles from full-text aggregators such as EBSCO, Gale, Lexis-Nexis, ProQuest, and Wilson. Thus our users had no single finding tool available for these rich sources of content. With these added to our Public Access Menu, our listed offerings exploded from about 4,200 titles to over 35,000 unique titles overnight!

Once the initial load was done, we found that ongoing maintenance of our database using Serials Solutions had its problems. With the very next datafeed from Serials Solutions, we found that dozens of publisher titles that we had activated as part of our implementation had dropped out. With help from Serials Solutions staff, we found out why. The most recent updates that Serials Solutions had received from these publishers had title records that didn't match up with those already in the Serials Solutions database. The unmatched records in the Serials Solutions database were thus deactivated, and dropped out of our profile. The "new" title records from the publishers' updates created new records for these titles in the Serials Solutions database, but our datafeed did not include them because these were not the records we had selected. With Serials Solutions' help, we reinstated these titles in our profile. Serials Solutions established controls for updating their database from publisher updates, and this didn't happen again.

Over time, we had other issues with the quality of the Serials Solutions datafeed. Serials Solutions is dependant in the first instance on getting good information from publishers. But, beyond that, we found for most publisher packages of any size that not all licensed titles are in Serials Solutions, and not all titles selectable for a publisher are necessarily part of the license. This means that each title in a large package (i.e., ScienceDirect, Kluwer, etc.) must be selected individually. And titles not represented in Serials Solutions must be dealt with manually in the local database or not at all.

For Elsevier and other publishers with deep backfile or other collection licensing options, selection in Serials Solutions of all licensed collections results in duplicate listings of titles. For Highwire and other publishers which offer free access for selected titles after an initial embargo period, the embargo period "End Date" was reflected in the datafeed, even for subscribed titles for which we had full access rights. At that time (and until early 2004), the Serials Solutions Client Center had no means to locally edit the "Start Date" or "End Date" of a title.

The most critical ongoing problem we faced, however, was the fact that the records contained in the datafeed from Serials Solutions have no unique identifier. Thus, the datafeed could not be taken and directly matched, record for record, against the local database. We also found that, with the issues we were finding with the data quality, we could not do unmediated updating of our database from the datafeed. Some publishers' title records in the raw datafeed required review and editing (sometimes extensive), before being processed into the database.

To overcome these problems, our Systems staff developed a record matching program which used a combination of the fields available (ISSN, Source, Title, etc.) to match the update records to the database records. Then, to allow a review of the update records (before actually changing the database records), Systems staff developed a series of Processing Reports (see Figure 4).

From this opening screen, the reviewer was able to select the appropriate report to:

1. Process either a publisher or an aggregator resource
2. Process from the Serials Solutions datafeed to the database:
   a. New records added (no matching record in database)
   b. Old records updated (records match, some information changed)
   c. Old records deleted (no matching record from datafeed)
   d. Old records not changed (records match perfectly)
   e. Unmatched records for review (multiple records from datafeed match single database record)
3. The review was able to update all records in a report, or update only selected records.

FIGURE 4. Serials Solutions Processing Reports Selection

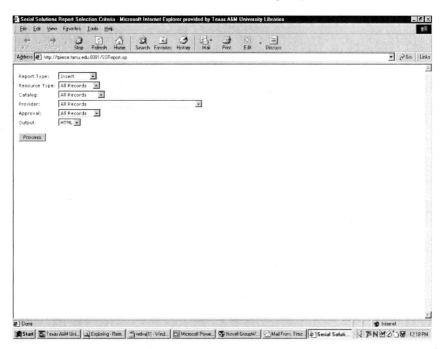

See Figure 5 for sample "Insert Report" screen for adding new records.

In early 2003, the Libraries committed to implement SFX. One question to be answered was whether we would continue to need a service such as Serials Solutions to augment the KnowledgeBase of SFX, or whether we would be able to manage our subscriptions fully within SFX. Because of our ongoing concerns with the quality and completeness of the Serials Solutions datafeed, I obtained trial data from EBSCO A-to-Z and from TDNet for 3 publishers (Elsevier, Kluwer and Wiley) and for 3 aggregators (Academic Search Premier, Lexis-Nexis Academic, and Wilson Omnifile Mega) (see Table 1).

A review of these numbers and the underlying title lists show that SFX is as comprehensive in its coverage as the other content tracking services. Primarily, what currently does drop out on SFX are titles with no ISSNs. The current version of SFX does not support records that have no ISSNs, but this support is expected to come with Version 3.

We found several features in SFX that help make subscription maintenance much more efficient. First, it includes the ability to set local "thresholds" for beginning date and ending date of coverage. SFX also allows the manual addition of titles which may be missing from a publisher portfolio. And one of the

FIGURE 5. Sample "Insert Report"

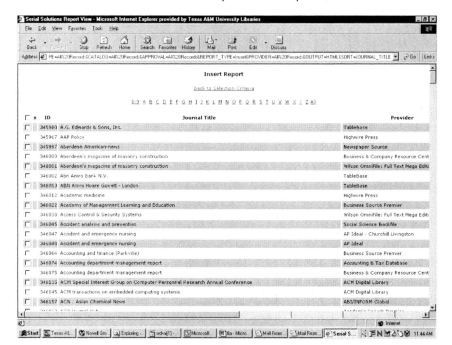

TABLE 1. Number of Records Supplied by Serials Solutions, EBSCO A-to-Z, TDNet, and SFX for 3 Aggregators and 3 Publishers

Aggregators	Serials Solutions	EBSCO A-to-Z	TDNet	SFX
Academic Search Premier	3,433	3,968	3,852	4,285
Lexis-Nexis Academic	4,373	5,872	5,636	1,696
Wilson Omnifile Mega	1,710	1,871	1,694	1,626
Publishers				
Elsevier	1,271	1,989	2,000	2,227
Kluwer	700	775	. 718	838
Wiley	421	449	449	466

best features is that the administrator screens for these functions provide for sending e-mail messages to the SFX helpdesk, which capture full information about the record being modified locally. It also includes a text block for a description of why the administrator made the change. In most cases, SFX can then correct their database and distribute the change globally with the next monthly update to its customers. With this reassurance concerning the completeness of the SFX KnowledgeBase, and the flexibility the system provides to add and modify records locally, we were quickly convinced that we had no need for a third party tracking service to augment SFX.

With the dramatic shift in usage from the print to the electronic, we have moved aggressively over the last 3 years to electronic only licensing from publishers which assure permanent access rights. This has included publishers such as Elsevier, IEEE, Kluwer, OECD, Wiley, and others. In some cases, the conversion to electronic only has financed the license itself, expanding our access to all the publisher's titles at little or no additional cost to the subscription base. In other cases, conversion to electronic helped blunt the overall inflation of serials. By 2004, our conversion to electronic only has affected over 3,000 titles.

This conversion has also allowed us to redirect our human resources. With more than a quarter of our subscriptions no longer coming in print format, and with more of the workload being related to electronic acquisitions, we have been able to shift 2 supporting staff positions from print-related activities to electronic. This reorganization and reorientation toward the electronic will be key to our continuing success in delivering electronic content and services to our users.

Can SFX Replace Your Homegrown Periodicals Holding List? How the University of Wisconsin-La Crosse Made the Transition

Jenifer S. Holman

SUMMARY. Ex Libris' SFX software is widely known for its context-sensitive linking capabilities, but it can also provide a searchable and browseable interface to a library's print and electronic journal holdings data. After five years of maintaining a homegrown Web-based periodicals holding database, Murphy Library has licensed SFX software and migrated all periodicals holdings information from its locally managed database to SFX. This article outlines the process of switching to this new system and some of the benefits of moving to an SFX environment. *[Article copies available for a fee from The Haworth Document Delivery Service: 1-800-HAWORTH. E-mail address: <docdelivery@haworthpress.com> Website: <http://www.HaworthPress.com> © 2005 by The Haworth Press, Inc. All rights reserved.]*

Jenifer S. Holman, MILS, is Acquisitions Librarian at Murphy Library, University of Wisconsin-La Crosse, 1631 Pine St., La Crosse, WI 54601 (E-mail: holman.jeni@ uwlax.edu).

The author wishes to thank Ex Libris for giving permission to include screenshots of the SFX administrative module in this paper and David Walker for sharing his SFX knowledge and his Visual Basic scripts.

[Haworth co-indexing entry note]: "Can SFX Replace Your Homegrown Periodicals Holding List? How the University of Wisconsin-La Crosse Made the Transition." Holman, Jenifer S. Co-published simultaneously in *The Serials Librarian* (The Haworth Information Press, an imprint of The Haworth Press, Inc.) Vol. 47, No. 4, 2005, pp. 79-88; and: *Electronic Journal Management Systems: Experiences from the Field* (ed: Gary Ives) The Haworth Information Press, an imprint of The Haworth Press, Inc., 2005, pp. 79-88. Single or multiple copies of this article are available for a fee from The Haworth Document Delivery Service [1-800-HAWORTH, 9:00 a.m. - 5:00 p.m. (EST). E-mail address: docdelivery@haworthpress.com].

KEYWORDS. SFX, journal management, union lists, case studies

BACKGROUND/INTRODUCTION–MURPHY LIBRARY

The University of Wisconsin-La Crosse's Murphy Library is part of the University of Wisconsin System, which is comprised of 13 four-year campuses and 13 two-year campuses.[1] Murphy Library is also a member of the UW-System's active library consortium. Holding over 1200 periodical subscriptions, Murphy Library also licenses nearly two hundred bibliographic databases. The full-text titles available through many of these aggregator databases account for another 15,000 constantly shifting journal titles. The need to provide accurate access to our journal titles has led us to search for new ways to manage access to all of our periodicals, regardless of format. Since 1999, the periodicals department staff has maintained an ASP-driven database that brought together print and electronic periodicals holdings data, as well as holdings data from La Crosse area libraries.

In 2003, a UW-System Electronic Resource Management Task Force was charged with selecting a federated searching/cross-linking software system for the campus libraries. After careful consideration and months of research, this task force chose Ex Libris' SFX and MetaLib. While we were excited about the context-sensitive linking that SFX would provide our users, we were most intrigued by the possibility that SFX's Citation Linker and A to Z features could replace our current periodicals database.

This paper chronicles our need for and creation of a homegrown periodicals database and how we are benefiting from our successful migration to an SFX Knowledge Base generated database.

PROVIDING ACCESS TO PERIODICALS

In late 1999, Murphy Library users accessed the journal collection primarily through the online catalog (Endeavor's Voyager) and secondarily through a printed holdings list. Although the catalog served as the authority for holdings data, users preferred access to our print and microform journal holdings through bound volumes known simply as the "orange book." One reason for the orange book's great popularity was the added value it provided as a local union list of periodicals, containing the local journal holdings from two hospital libraries, three college libraries, and our local public library. Users also found it very convenient to quickly flip through the pages as they scanned citations from their bibliographic searches and view all the local holdings for a particular title at once. Several major problems, however, existed with this printed list: (1) it was updated, bound, and distributed only once a year; (2) a work-study student spent an entire summer of editing to manually check and update changes from our local libraries, and; (3) the beautifully bound list was nearly obsolete–especially with regard to electronic full-text holdings–as soon as it was printed. In addition to maintenance problems, by the fall of 2000, library users had access to over 15,000 full-text titles through our licensed databases and online subscriptions and we simply did not have the manpower to include these holdings in the orange book (or even in our catalog). This problem led to a search for an efficient way to provide access to this new wealth of journal information without adding thousands of records to our catalog.

Later that same year, after reading a pivotal article by Gary Roberts[2] about using a simple Microsoft Access database to create a searchable listing of periodicals holdings on the Web, a small group comprised of the systems librarian, the periodicals librarian, and a student intern with programming skills began working on our own Web-enabled database solution. Within a year we had a simple Microsoft Access database Web running on our campus web server utilizing Microsoft's Active Server Pages (ASP) scripting environment. Our periodicals holdings list database included not only the print holdings from local libraries, but full-text electronic journal holdings from our aggregator databases as well. The interface featured simple keyword searching, browsing by title, an ISSN search, and the ability to limit searches by owning library or format (Figure 1).

The success of our new database driven holdings list was evident, when on February 11, 2000, Murphy librarians voted unanimously in favor of no longer publishing the printed orange book and relying solely on the online periodicals holdings list. Although our users and the librarians found the periodicals holdings list easy to use and very convenient, the behind the scenes work spent maintaining and enhancing the search interface and keeping the data updated was substantial. Each month, we extracted data from our Voyager ILS and downloaded updated holdings information from our aggregator database vendors. While our database vendors maintain publicly available title lists that we

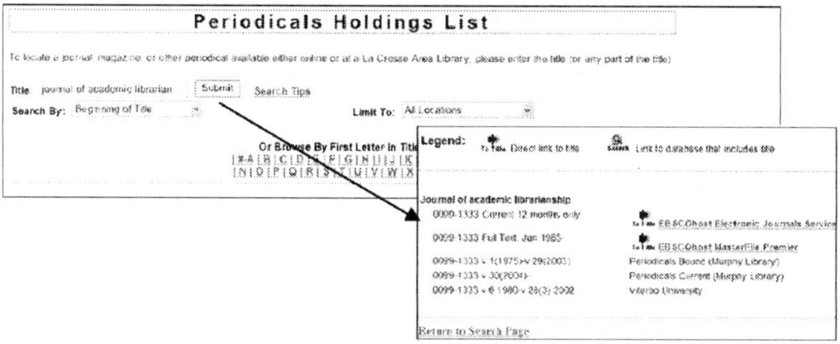

FIGURE 1. Murphy Library's Homegrown Periodicals Holdings List

were able to download each month, each vendor formats their holdings differently, requiring many hours of staff time manipulating the data into the format required for our local database. Each summer, our local libraries sent us their holdings data updates which we also configured. The work involved in updating our local database gave us valuable experience in manipulating data and a greater sense of control over our holdings, but we quickly realized the shortcomings of our system, especially in terms of the time commitment needed to keep the database current.

As much of an advancement as the periodicals holding list was, users still performed a separate search to locate journal holdings within the periodical holdings list after completing their initial bibliographic search. One frustrating aspect of this design was that users frequently discovered, after all their searching, that the journal they needed was not available locally. Another design issue was limited title authority control; each library and vendor uses a slightly different title variation and we had no system in place to bring those variations under control. By 2004 both librarians and users sought a better solution to the problem of accessing journal holdings than our homegrown periodicals database offered.

SOLUTION: SFX

The UW-System task force could not have licensed SFX at a better time, as we were quickly outgrowing our simple periodicals holdings list database and in need of a more robust way to link users with content. Even before the ink dried on the contract with Ex Libris, librarians at Murphy Library began contemplating how SFX could replace our homegrown periodicals database and help reduce staff time involved in updating journal holdings. After our formal SFX training in March 2004 and a brief period of internal testing, we went live with SFX in May 2004 in order to test in a real-world environment. While enabling our databases to communicate with the SFX server and activating our licensed databases in the SFX administrative module was a very straight forward process, we spent another month thinking how we could best utilize the powerful SFX environment to replace our periodicals holdings list database.

SFX offers two options for searching a library's subscribed/licensed titles in the SFX Knowledge Base. The first option is an A to Z list that is generated through the SFX administrative module (Figure 2). The A to Z list is completely customizable (administrators can specify which targets–groups of titles–to include) and integrates easily with a library's local Web server. Although we have not customized our A to Z list yet, the default list contains all the information that we provided in our local database, and offers the benefit of complete title authority control.

The second option is called Citation Linker, which is a search interface for the SFX Knowledge Base (Figure 3).

The SFX Citation Linker is a much more robust searching environment than our periodicals holdings list database as it allows users to search not only for a journal title or ISSN, but by article and issue level details as well. While the Citation Linker is ultimately a more advanced search interface than our local database, one important Citation Linker shortcoming we have found is the

FIGURE 2. SFX Default A to Z List

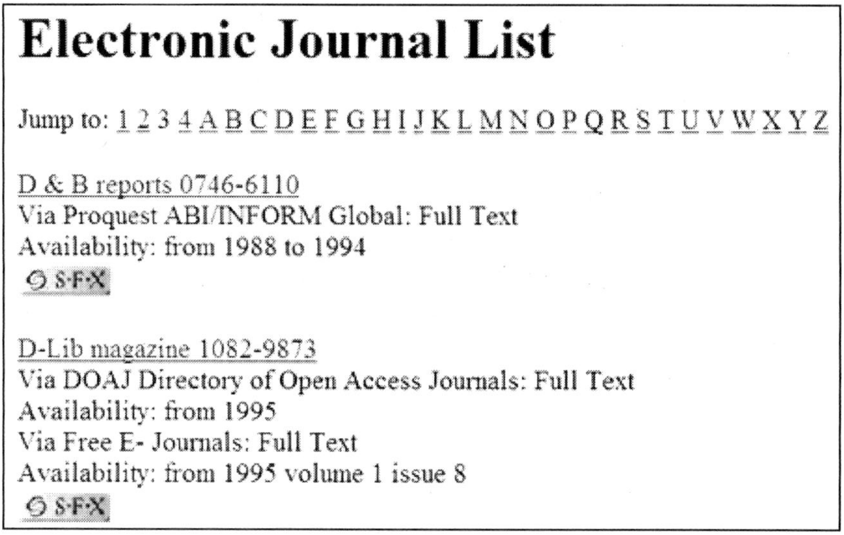

Electronic Journal List

Jump to: 1 2 3 4 A B C D E F G H I J K L M N O P Q R S T U V W X Y Z

D & B reports 0746-6110
Via Proquest ABI/INFORM Global: Full Text
Availability: from 1988 to 1994
SFX

D-Lib magazine 1082-9873
Via DOAJ Directory of Open Access Journals: Full Text
Availability: from 1995
Via Free E- Journals: Full Text
Availability: from 1995 volume 1 issue 8
SFX

FIGURE 3. SFX Citation Linker

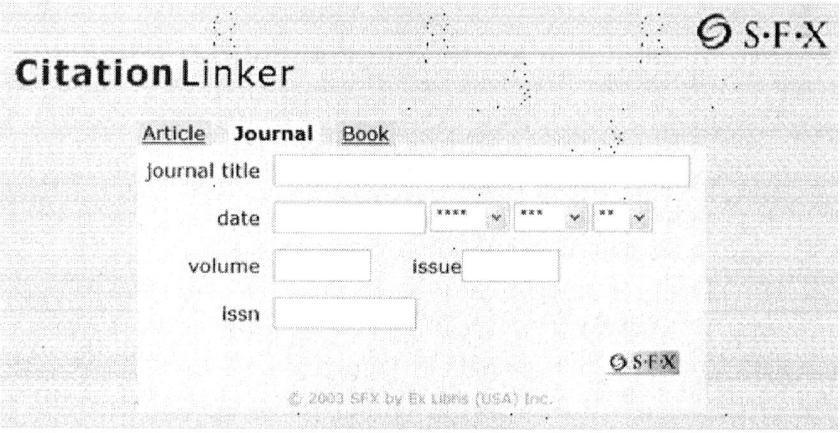

Citation Linker   S·F·X

Article **Journal** Book

journal title [   ]

date [   ] [**** v] [*** v] [** v]

volume [   ]   issue [   ]

issn [   ]

SFX

© 2003 SFX by Ex Libris (USA) Inc.

necessity of searching for an exact title. If users do not enter the exact journal title or happen to misspell a word, SFX will return a default list of services available for any title in the SFX database, even if it is not locally held and even if the
title may have been available full text if it had been spelled right (Figure 4).

In a recent communication to its customers at the annual meeting of their
user group,[3] Ex Libris has announced, however, that the next release of SFX
(version 3) will include keyword searching (contains, begins with, and exact
match) in the Citation Linker. Keyword searching would lead users to a list of
titles alphabetically adjacent to their search, helping users to pinpoint spelling
problems. Currently, by using the percentage character (%) as a truncation
symbol, users can bring back the first ten titles (and only those first ten titles)
in the SFX knowledge base that contain the search term, but the Citation
Linker currently works best when users enter an exact title.

Once we had activated the holdings of our aggregator databases and electronic
journal subscriptions, our electronic journals were searchable within the Citation
Linker (as well as within all the databases that are OpenURL compliant). When
the SFX global knowledge base is updated each month, we receive reports regarding any changes that vendors have made in their data. We selected the option to
have these updates automatically applied to our aggregator databases, another important benefit of SFX that enables our staff to focus on other projects.

MIGRATING PRINT AND UNION LIST HOLDINGS

While configuring SFX to manage access to our electronic journal holdings
was a simple process, migrating our print holdings and our union list holdings

FIGURE 4. Search Results from a Misspelled Title

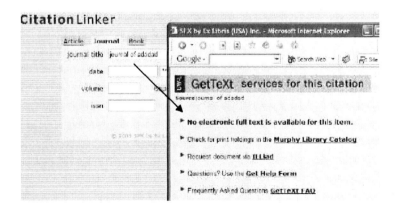

held additional challenges. The default SFX interaction with print holdings is through a Z39.50 search of a library's catalog. Although administrators can control many of the services that appear in the menu based on their availability, SFX cannot determine whether a library owns a local copy until users instruct the software to perform a Z39.50 search and display the results. If users then choose to search the catalog, a new window opens displaying the search results, which can frequently include nothing more than a short error message indicating "no items found." Since our local print/microform journal holdings had always been a part of our local database, we did not want our users to have to search our catalog separately for these holdings data.

Since the strength of SFX is its context-sensitive search results, we decided to download the print and microform holdings from our catalog and then upload these data into SFX. Once the holdings were loaded into the SFX Knowledge Base, users would only see the holdings in the SFX menu if they matched data from the specific citation for which they were searching. The biggest challenge we faced at this point was that SFX needs holdings data coded in PERL statements rather than MARC formatted summary holdings statements. David Walker at California State University at San Marcos presented us with an elegant solution to this problem of how to quickly convert our MARC holding statements into SFX PERL holding statements. Walker's Web site[4] contains a wealth of practical advice for those new to SFX. Walker's "Local Print Collections" page includes several solutions for handling local holdings, and Walker's jholding script proved to be the right solution for Murphy Library. Written in Visual Basic, the script takes data extracted from the catalog (ISSN and holdings data) and transforms them into SFX's PERL format.

Once data were successfully parsed through the jholdings program, they were uploaded to their appropriate target via the SFX DataLoader tool (Figure 5).

After we had loaded the data, our holdings displayed properly in the services menu. Although running our holdings through the jholdings script seemed to be an easy process, we quickly discovered the importance of error checking. If there was an error in the PERL syntax of our holding statement, the holdings simply would not appear in the services menu. Once we realized the importance of proper syntax, we were able to utilize another SFX tool, the Threshold Tool (Figure 6), to quickly locate the malformed holdings statements.

This tool checks syntax for the titles within a given target service and then creates a tab-delimited text file listing any errors. We were often able to correct multiple mistakes at once using a simple find and replace command, then resend the cleaned up data file back to the SFX database through the DataLoader. SFX includes a strong error checking and handling system that has already proved invaluable in our initial interaction with the software. While David Walker's jholding program encountered some difficulties with our MARC holdings, the process helped us uncover some formatting issues with our holdings. The majority of our holdings were loaded successfully into SFX. Currently, SFX can only load titles that include an ISSN into the Knowl-

FIGURE 5. SFX DataLoader

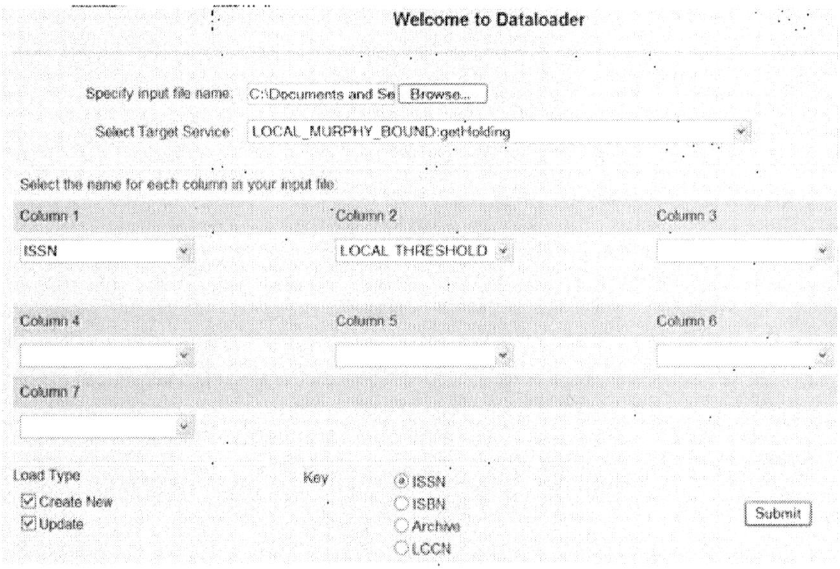

Welcome to Dataloader

Specify input file name: C:\Documents and Se [Browse...]

Select Target Service: LOCAL_MURPHY_BOUND:getHolding

Select the name for each column in your input file:

Column 1	Column 2	Column 3
ISSN	LOCAL THRESHOLD	

Column 4	Column 5	Column 6

Column 7

Load Type   Key   ⦿ ISSN
☑ Create New   ○ ISBN
☑ Update   ○ Archive   [Submit]
                               ○ LCCN

FIGURE 6. SFX Threshold Tool

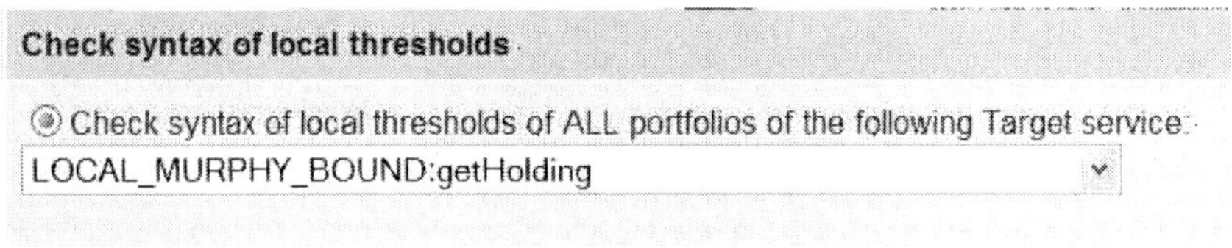

Check syntax of local thresholds

⦿ Check syntax of local thresholds of ALL portfolios of the following Target service:
LOCAL_MURPHY_BOUND:getHolding

edge Base. Ex Libris is developing a solution to this issue, but our titles without ISSN numbers cannot be loaded into the Knowledge Base at this time. Figure 7 illustrates how our local holdings display in the SFX services menu.

Users now see our holdings at a glance, and they have the option to click on the associated link to run a catalog search for that title and view the complete catalog record. We anticipate that our new periodicals database interface (Figure 8) will go live in fall 2004.

CONCLUSION

Librarians at Murphy Library are very excited about moving to this new SFX-powered journal locator. Users will benefit from context-sensitive link-

FIGURE 7. SFX Service Menu

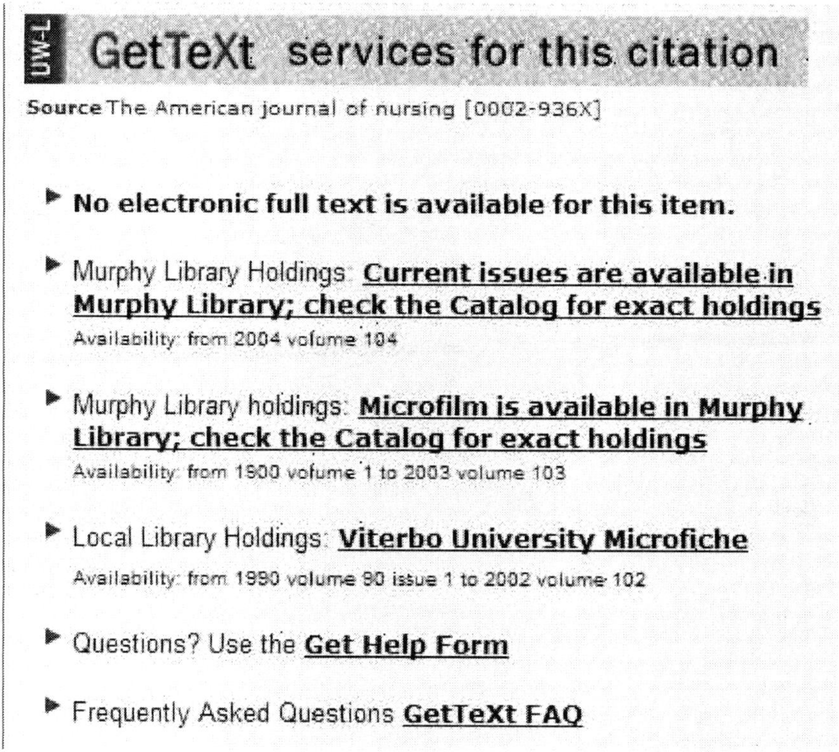

FIGURE 8. Murphy Library's SFX Generated Journal Locator

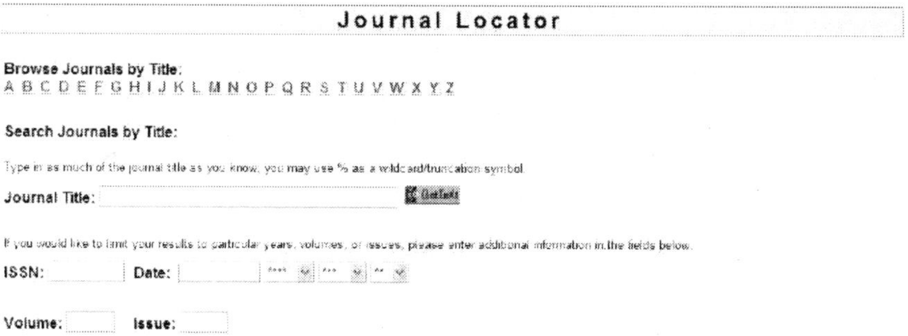

ing and only view holdings from other area libraries if Murphy Library cannot provide the item. When none of our area libraries holds a needed item, users can select a link to our interlibrary loan system (ILLiad) from the SFX menu and login to an interlibrary loan form that already includes information about their request filled in for them. Managing our journal locator via SFX will save staff time and will provide our users with a richer array of information at their point of need–both within the search results of their bibliographic searches and as a separately searchable database.

NOTES

1. University of Wisconsin. (2003-2004). Fact Book. http://www.uwsa.edu/univ_rel/publicat/factbook2003.pdf (accessed July 16, 2004).

2. Gary Roberts, "Constructing a Database of Local Serials Holdings," *Computers in Libraries* 19, no.9 (1999): 24-35.

3. Lieve Rottiers, "SFX Version 3" (Paper presented at the annual meeting of the SFX/MetaLib Users Group, Boston, June 2004.) https://www.exlibrisgroup.com/docs (accessed July 30, 2004).

4. David Walker, "CSU SFX MetaLib Resource Web Site." http://library.csusm.edu/csu/ (accessed July 16, 2004).

Customized Electronic Resources Management System for a Multi-Library University: Viewpoint from One Library

Janis F. Brown
Janet L. Nelson
Maggie Wineburgh-Freed

SUMMARY. The University of Southern California's multiple library systems function like a consortia rather than a single entity. The libraries required a system that serves multiple purposes including creating Web

Janis F. Brown, MLS, is Associate Director, Systems and Information Technology, Norris Medical Library, University of Southern California, 2003 Zonal Avenue, Los Angeles, CA 90089-9130 (E-mail: jbrown@usc.edu).

Janet L. Nelson, MLS, is Associate Director, Education and Research Services, Norris Medical Library, University of Southern California, 2003 Zonal Avenue, Los Angeles, CA 90089-9130 (E-mail: janetnel@usc.edu).

Maggie Wineburgh-Freed, MSLS, is Head, Technical Services Section, Norris Medical Library, University of Southern California, 2003 Zonal Avenue, Los Angeles, CA 90089-9130 (E-mail: mwfreed@usc.edu).

This was a joint project of the University of Southern California Information Services Division Libraries and the Health Sciences Libraries and also involved considerable effort by Louise Marks, Web programmer, and Marianne Afifi, Director of Electronic Resources and Special Projects Development, both from ISD.

[Haworth co-indexing entry note]: "Customized Electronic Resources Management System for a Multi-Library University: Viewpoint from One Library." Brown, Janis F., Janet L. Nelson, and Maggie Wineburgh-Freed. Co-published simultaneously in *The Serials Librarian* (The Haworth Information Press, an imprint of The Haworth Press, Inc.) Vol. 47, No. 4, 2005, pp. 89-102; and: *Electronic Journal Management Systems: Experiences from the Field* (ed: Gary Ives) The Haworth Information Press, an imprint of The Haworth Press, Inc., 2005, pp. 89-102. Single or multiple copies of this article are available for a fee from The Haworth Document Delivery Service [1-800-HAWORTH, 9:00 a.m. - 5:00 p.m. (EST). E-mail address: docdelivery@haworthpress.com].

http://www.haworthpress.com/web/SER
Digital Object Identifier: 10.1300/J123v47n04_10

pages, sharing resources, and managing licensed resources. To meet all the needs and to deal with the issue of each library using different library systems, the libraries created a customized database. Librarians from the multiple systems and a Web programmer worked as a team to develop the database. Although the smaller partner in the project, the Health Sciences Libraries played a vital role and achieved a system that met its individual needs. *[Article copies available for a fee from The Haworth Document Delivery Service: 1-800-HAWORTH. E-mail address: <docdelivery@ haworthpress.com> Website: <http://www.HaworthPress.com> © 2005 by The Haworth Press, Inc. All rights reserved.]*

KEYWORDS. Electronic journal management, electronic resources management

HEALTH SCIENCES LIBRARIES ENVIRONMENT

The Health Sciences Libraries (HSL), one of three library systems at the University of Southern California, supports the health sciences schools and clinical programs. The Information Services Division (ISD) includes all the other libraries in the university except the Law Library. Each of the systems is administratively separate. The systems maintain different library applications including integrated library systems (ILS), but they cooperate in collection development so that resources purchased for one library system are available to the entire university. In some cases, both ISD and HSL provide funds to purchase a particular resource or collection. In other cases, both systems purchase their own copy of a resource. The library systems work together in many ways like a consortium.

HSL uses Dynix Horizon for its ILS, Majors Scientific Books for book purchases, and Swets Information Services for journal subscriptions. SFX is used for article link resolving primarily with Ovid MEDLINE and PubMed. HSL purchases most of its electronic journals directly from publishers rather than from aggregators or databases with full text. Its main database vendor is Ovid through which it purchases licenses for about 330 electronic journals and 60 electronic books.

The libraries' Web site, NMLweb, includes pages of licensed resources, as well as freely available Web sites that the librarians have selected as being of value to the health sciences community. The OPAC includes all licensed resources and has separate records for print and electronic versions of the same title. The HSL OPAC includes a few selected Web sites, such as the *USMLE (United States Medical Licensing Examination)* and *FREIDA Online (Fellowship and Residency Electronic Interactive Database Access System)*, but not the majority of sites included on NMLweb. The library has approximately 2920 electronic resources, of which about 1450 are licensed electronic journals and 120 are licensed electronic books.

NEED FOR AN ELECTRONIC RESOURCES MANAGEMENT SYSTEM

HSL had several needs for a new electronic resources management system. HSL and ISD had been using a database approach for populating their Web sites of electronic resources since early 1999. The old system required each library system to maintain its own separate database. The Macintosh FileMaker Pro and Lasso system was successful in generating static pages, but it had limited search capabilities for users and included minimal data for licensed electronic resource control. The university also needed to port the database to the university's standard hardware and software, namely a MySQL database manipulated by PHP on a UNIX server.

The libraries wanted to develop a combined database for all of the university's electronic resources that would allow for more sharing between the library systems, as well as provide a means for users to search all the resources at once, if desired.

Also, perhaps most critical, as the number of electronic journals acquired exploded, HSL needed a database solution to manage licensed electronic resources. The paper management systems were no longer functional, as dealing with electronic resources often required multiple library staff to look up information about a specific resource simultaneously. Technical services staff also needed to input similar data in multiple places and did not have an easy method for tracking the data.

The USC libraries have long realized the utility of a databased approach to generating Web sites[1] as advocated by Sitko[2] and Rich.[3] The libraries had several compelling needs for developing an in-house database of electronic resources, rather than using commercial sources as described by Watson.[4] The USC libraries use their Web sites to provide user access to all electronic resources, not just electronic journals. The libraries want to provide not only an alphabetical list of all electronic journals, but also lists by subject that included relevant resources in all formats. Since the libraries needed a solution that encompassed more than electronic journals, most commercial products, of which few were available when this project began in 2002, were unsatisfactory. At this time the HSL ILS, Dynix Horizon, still does not provide electronic resource control. Further, the goal of creating one database for the entire university is complicated by the existence of different integrated library systems for each library system. For these many reasons, an in-house development was deemed the best approach. The availability of the Web programmer who had developed the earlier database made the decision easier.

The overall goals of the electronic resources database were (1) to provide a means for creating Web pages of electronic resources with the flexibility of generating static pages as well as dynamic pages as a result of a custom search, (2) to manage and control electronic resources in a database, and (3) to create one database for use by both library systems for sharing resources and for allowing users to search most university resources at once.

DATABASE DEVELOPMENT

Key players from each library system worked together with the Web programmer to determine needs, specify tables and the elements of each table. The group built on the work of other academic libraries including UCLA, Washington State University, and the Tri-College Consortium (Bryn Mawr, Haverford, and Swarthmore colleges) with similar electronic resources databases identified from Chandler and Jewell's Web site.[5] By reviewing the tables and elements in use by others, the group was able quickly to determine the relevant ones. Since the programmer had developed the earlier database she was familiar with the overall concepts involved, but additional details were provided regarding the interrelationships of the new tables for vendor, license, and gateway. For example, she needed to know that one title might be provided through multiple gateways, so it might need different URLs and different holdings dates.

Each library system specified its own public search interface and results displays, as well as agreed upon elements for a search of all resources combined. Each library system also created its own lists of broad subject categories. Additional needs were identified as the development proceeded, and the librarians were able to test the various modules.

The programmer divided the project into two phases, with the first phase focused on developing a system with at least the same functionality as the previous database. She deemed some requests as Phase II projects that will be dealt with some time in the future. But the resulting Phase I database is a vast improvement over the earlier database and has many excellent features.

DATABASE DESCRIPTION

The database content includes paid licensed resources, free Web sites, and all remote electronic formats including books, databases, and journals. Unfortunately, the electronic resources database is not a comprehensive solution for the HSL or ISD. For HSL, electronic journal management still requires duplication of entry for some data, as payment and renewal information is processed and made available for viewing through Swets Information Services' customer database, DataswetsConnect. Payment information for electronic books and databases is maintained in the ILS. Article link resolving also is managed outside the electronic resources database. Electronic journal holdings are added to SFX and also to Ovid JCodes for display as a local holdings statement. As a health sciences library, HSL also adds all journal holdings information to the DOCLINE serial holdings database at the National Library of Medicine for routing of interlibrary loan material.

The electronic resources relational database includes five tables to describe the unique resource and other information including vendor, gateway, and license that could be used to describe multiple resources. Figure 1 shows the interrelationships among the tables. In other words, as with all relational databases, when there was a one-to-one or one-to-many relationship a separate table was defined. Resource and title records are required for each item. Free Web resources do not have vendor, license nor gateway information. One database is used for both library systems, but it is used to create separate Web sites for each of the libraries with different resources for each site described by different subject categories and other features unique to each library. Each library retains "ownership" of items input, and by default those items appear on the different library Web sites. However, each library may also mark a re-

FIGURE 1. Electronic resources database tables and interrelationships.

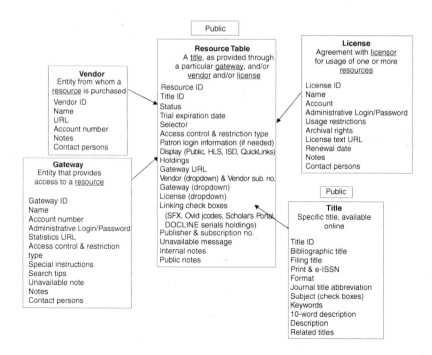

source belonging to the other to appear on its Web site and add subject terms and other information appropriate for its own collection. This capability of creating library-specific pages is especially important for HSL since the database includes many more resources "owned" by ISD of which most are of little interest to health sciences users.

The resource table describes a unique item and connects that resource to the other tables through the title ID, vendor ID, gateway ID, and the license ID when appropriate. This table includes information vital to the public search and display of records such as inclusion in ISD and HSL Web sites, the resource URL and holdings, access restriction specifications (e.g., IP recognition, logon, etc.), passwords for qualified users when required (which will be available through an IP domain-restricted page in phase II of the project), and hiding the resource from public display in the event that it is temporarily unavailable, with a note for public display. The resource table also includes management information such as vendor and publisher names, tracking of links in other systems (e.g., Ovid JCodes, SFX, Scholar's Portal), and status of the resource (e.g., active, trial, suspended). Identification of the resource selector is also included allowing for administrative searches for all resources selected by a specific librarian.

The title table appears with the resource table as shown in Figures 2 and 3 for administrative inputting purposes. For the many Web sites that are not licensed, but are selected for the library Web site, this title/resource input form is the only one required. The title table includes the bibliographic descriptive elements for each item that are required for identification purposes and for the public search and display, such as title, filing title, journal title abbreviation, title annotations, related titles, and ISSNs. Subjects from a controlled list of broad topics and formats (journal, book, Web site, database) are assigned, as well as more specific keywords. A controlled list of keywords is provided that contains more specific terms that can be changed more easily than the broad subjects list. A paragraph description field is also included. Since each library system uses different broad subject topics, the appropriate subject terms appear on the input form as check boxes depending upon the maintainer's affiliation. Because some predefined aggregations are purchased, the libraries receive some duplicate titles from different vendors. In these cases, the title links to more than one resource and the various gateways and licensing guidelines will be displayed.

The vendor table is for internal electronic resource management purposes only. It includes account number, administration username and password, and contact persons for the company from which a resource is ordered, such as Swets or Nature for journals, and Stat!Ref for books. Since the resource records are tied to the vendors, the administration input form for a specific vendor provides a list of the resources purchased through that vendor. The resource titles are live links allowing immediate access to the resource record.

FIGURE 2. Resource section of Resource/Title input form.

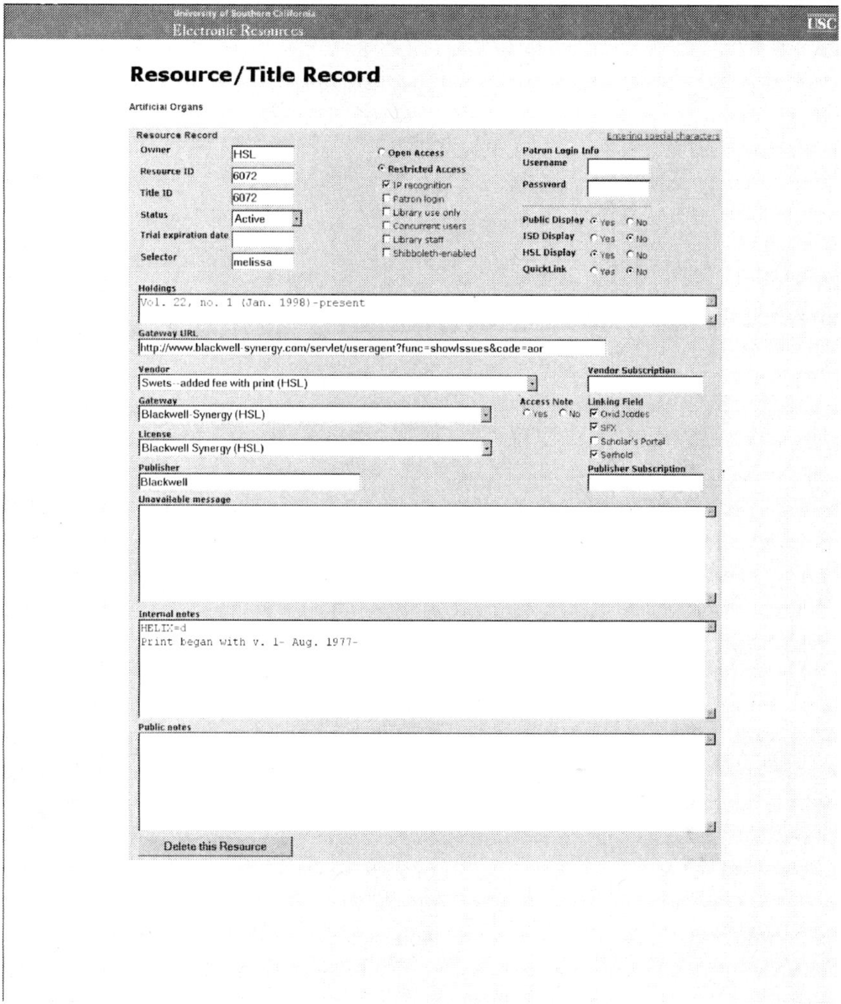

The gateway defines access for a resource. Gateways such as Ingenta, HighWire, and Extenza provide Web sites that multiple publishers use for providing access to their resources. The gateway table includes information that is used internally, as well as for the public listings of resources. A checkbox specifies the various options for access control, e.g., IP recognition, username

FIGURE 3. Title section of Resource/Title input form.

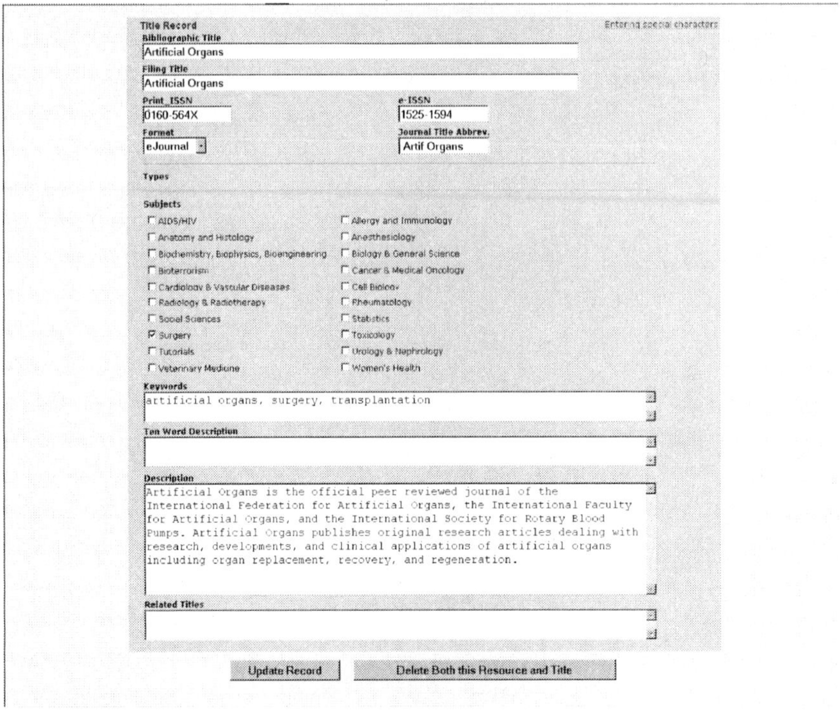

and password, library staff only, etc.; another field is used to generate a "USC only" icon for licensed resources; special instructions and search tips are provided; and a "temporarily unavailable" notation for users is included as an easy method of notifying users if a problem affects all resources accessed through a specific gateway. Other information for internal management related to a specific gateway, such as account number, administration username and password, contact people, etc., are also included.

The license table describes usage restrictions, archival rights and other administrative data such as license account number, administration username and password, contact person, renewal dates, and a link to the text of the license agreement. This information is for internal electronic resource control and management and is especially useful for document delivery services staff. The license agreements can be scanned into PDF files and placed on the library's intranet for easy access through the database. More succinct license usage restrictions are summarized and included in the "usage restrictions" field that will display on the public view for access services staff and faculty.

One license may apply to many resources and is tied to the resource record through the license ID number. For example, the ScienceDirect license is tied to the many journals purchased through Elsevier.

ADMINISTRATIVE FUNCTIONS

On the top-level administration site, electronic resource maintainers can perform quick searches for existing resources, vendors, gateways, or licenses. A more complex option as shown in Figure 4 also is available allowing searches of more fields (adding ISSN, format, subjects, description, selector, status, and owner, public display, and expiration date) in combination with each other, and with drop-down menus for fields that are predefined, such as format or subject, or can be populated from the database, such as vendor. Searches result in a list of titles indicating library affiliation, i.e., either HSL or ISD, with links to the resource/title input form.

Maintainers also can add new items to the database. Since resources can be distinct from titles, the administration site offers the possibility of either creating a new resource from an existing title or creating a new title/resource record.

FIGURE 4. Administrative quick search page.

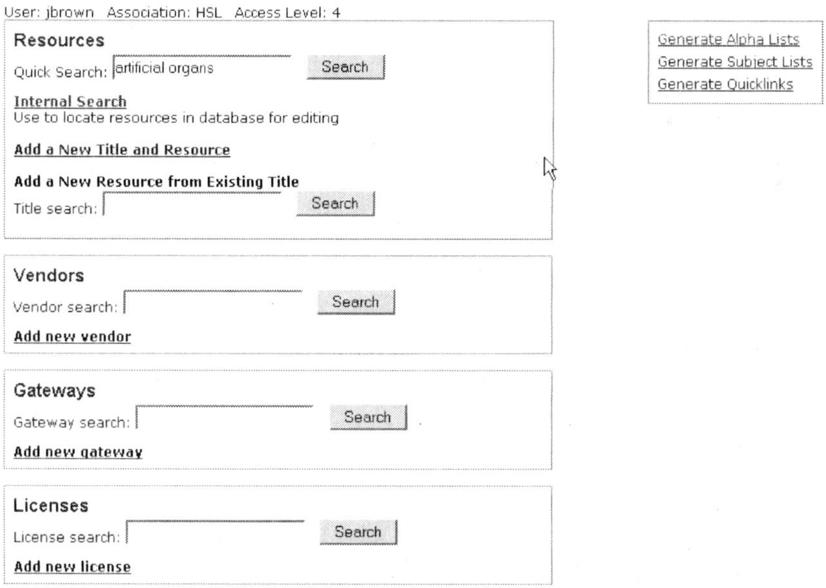

Each input form has an "update" button to modify a record. These changes are made immediately to the database. In addition, the administration site provides "generate" buttons for generating new static lists of electronic resources arranged either A to Z or by general subject category. In addition, QuickLinks of high demand items specified in the resource table also can be generated. A deleting record option is included on each of the different input forms. For the resource/title input form, maintainers may either delete the resource only or both the resource and title. A warning appears before deletions are complete, an especially important feature when deleting gateways and licenses!

The separate tables in this relational database make updating changes for vendors, gateways, and licenses easy, since the change can be made globally. For example, a change at the gateway level affects all the individual resources accessed through that specific gateway. The database input forms provide check boxes and pull-down menus for many fields, so that inputting is streamlined, the information displayed on the public site is uniform, and information for internal controls is consistent to make searching and report generating more reliable. The pull-down menus for vendors, gateways, and licenses are created from their respective tables, for example, a new vendor specified in the vendor table automatically appears in the resource/title table pull-down menu for vendors. Pubcookie, the open access intra-institutional Web authentication server, is used to control access to the administrative pages. Users of the database are assigned one of two access levels. Most database maintainers only need access to the resource/title input forms. Only a few require access to all the input forms since they relate primarily to licensed resources. These levels of authorization reduce errors in critical tables such as licenses, vendors, and gateways that could affect many resources in the database, and they also restrict access to sensitive data, such as vendor and gateway administration usernames and passwords. The database users also are associated with a specific library system, so they are restricted to modifying records owned by their library system except for the title/resource tables. For these tables, either library can "grab" a record owned by the other system to facilitate sharing without re-keying. However, each system can add its own subject and keyword terms to allow for individuality.

PUBLIC INTERFACE

The database search and display functionality is provided through a PHP script that is composed of some files such as the navigation that can be edited and other files such as the search code that cannot be modified. This modularity allows the database site to be inserted into the library Web site design,[6] so the look and feel remains consistent. As shown in Figure 5, users can search by keyword, title, or broad subject; select formats from checkbox options; and then choose either a brief list or full description display of results. The HSL's

FIGURE 5. Public search page for Norris Medical Library of the Health Sciences Libraries system.

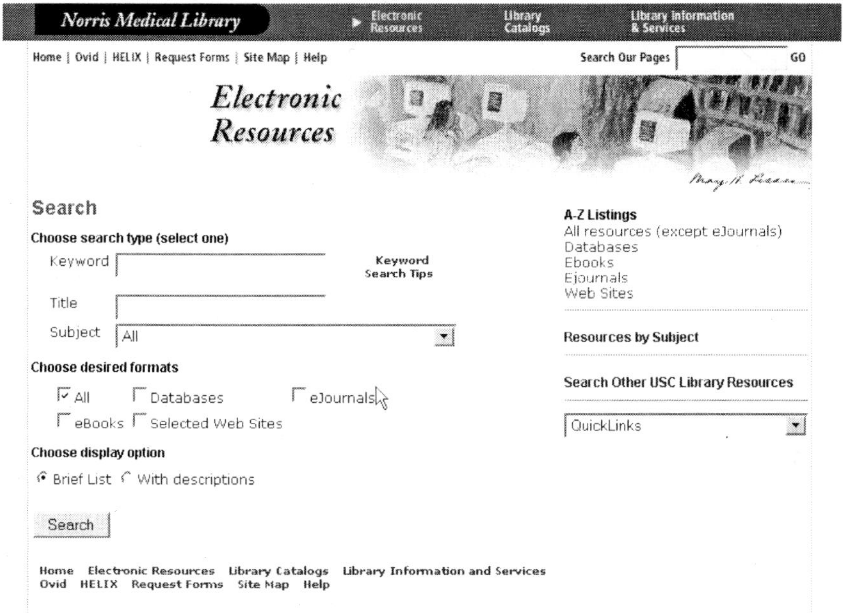

approximately 60 broad subjects are selected from a pull-down menu. A link to the keyword list also is provided as a guide; however, the keyword search includes words from keyword, title, title annotation, and resource description fields, so users may use free-text searching. The keyword option is listed first as we felt it is the most commonly used search. Defaults are set for searching all subject categories and all format types, and for brief list display of results. For example, users can type "evidence" in the keyword box with no other specifications, or they can also select "databases" as a format. This page allows for dynamic searches closely tailored to specific user requirements.

The search results pages are displayed either as a brief list or a list with descriptions. The results are listed by format in the order of books, databases, Web sites, other formats, and journals. The brief list includes a title that links to the resource, a title annotation when the title is not sufficient to describe the resource, holdings statements for journals, and a link to a More Info page that provides a paragraph description of the resource. When a title (primarily journals) has multiple gateways for access, then all gateways with holdings statements are included. A USC icon appears to the left of titles that are licensed for USC users only. The list with descriptions includes the same components and arrangement, but in addition includes the first fifty words of the More Info description. Some of the More Info descriptions are a very brief sentence, while others may be several paragraphs. The search results pages also include a vertical navigation bar that leads users back to the search functions and browse lists, as well as additional navigation points for electronic journals and databases. These navigation bars also include links to information on accessing licensed resources for valid users connecting from outside the university network and guidelines on electronic resource use and abuse.

The library electronic resources Web site also provides A to Z lists for browsing by format (journal, books, databases, and all resources except journals) and by broad subjects. These lists for browsing are static pages that are generated for predefined searches that would be in high demand. These pages, such as all electronic journals, are also fairly lengthy, so a static page will appear more quickly and reliably than from a dynamic search as described by Boiko.[7] Data maintainers can re-generate the lists as necessary after records have been added or changed. The browse lists follow the brief list formatting conventions.

ROLES AND RESPONSIBILITIES

The development of the electronic resources database was a team effort of librarians from both library systems along with a Web database programmer. For the HSL components, the database is maintained by a team of librarians and library staff from various units. Librarians, primarily those who serve reference functions, are assigned a topic area to maintain. They maintain resource and title information for unlicensed Web sites. The librarian who manages the technical services section and an electronic resources library assistant are responsible for the licensed resources and also have access to input forms for vendors, gateways, and licenses. Other librarians and staff assist as needed. Additional assistance was especially necessary during the transition period from the old database to the new one. Since each library system can share resources from the other system, communication is required to ensure that the title/resource information suits the purposes of both systems.

The Web programmer designed the database and developed the PHP scripts for the Web interactions for both public users and internal database maintainers. She is part of the Information Services Division's Web Services unit that offers fee-based services to the university. Since part of the Web Services budget provides support for the ISD Web site, most of the work was covered through that funding source. Web Services and the ISD libraries are sister units under the umbrella organization that includes computing, libraries, and telecommunications. The HSL contributed funds for work that was specifically for it, such as the public search interface and display pages. The Web programmer provides ongoing support with funding from both library systems.

FUTURE POSSIBILITIES AND CONCLUSIONS

One of the primary motivations for developing this electronic resources database was to replace an old database that was developed with software and hardware that was no longer supported. As part of Phase II, we would like to be able to generate reports of various kinds, such as titles by gateway and titles by librarian selector, without needing to call upon the Web programmer. Although statistics based on clicks to the resource are not a complete reflection of the use, these types of statistics have been useful with the previous database because they provided use relative to other resources. The statistics for the major licensed resources are probably most inaccurate, as users are likely to bookmark the resources accessed most frequently. However, these high demand resources also are most apt to have statistics provided by vendors. In the past, we have used the statistics to identify resources that are rarely used and have removed them from the database. We also want more control over the management of the database, for example, adding and deleting broad subject categories without requiring the programmer's intervention.

The immediate effect of the new database in technical services was to enable HSL to move from a paper-based system to an online system. Initially all staff worked to transfer to the new database information from the printed worksheets that were in use to maintain management data. Having this information accessible electronically allows several staff members to consult records simultaneously and prevents the frequent search for worksheets on desks and in personal files. After the initial transition to the new database, the effort of other librarians in maintaining the database has not changed substantially from the work on the earlier system. Information services librarians generally spend approximately one hour per week on maintaining their topic areas. An advantage of the new system is that resources shared by both systems only need to be updated by the owner. With the past system, the library systems had to communicate changes to each other and then duplicate the updating for each database.

The electronic resources database meets the originally stated goals of having a databased approach to creating Web pages of electronic resources, of being able to share resources with the other library systems, and having a database to manage electronic resources. The database is not a complete system solving all needs, but it provides us with a system that is much improved over the earlier one. The university libraries continue to look for other solutions, such as a collection information systems and new integrated library systems, to solve electronic resources management and control issues, so the current system is likely a temporary solution. Another unresolved problem is a single search for all electronic journals at the university. ISD maintains access to those journals available through aggregators and databases through Serials Solutions and not in the electronic resources database.

The in-house development of the electronic resources database has allowed for complete customization based on our needs. The library systems have not been constrained by the limitations often imposed by commercial solutions needing to meet the requirements of many institutions. However, the expertise of the Web programmer was an essential element for the successful development of this system. The HSL is a much smaller library system in terms of staff, overall budget, and other typical library measures. However, the HSL librarians were able to design a system that meets their needs by actively participating in the process; by having cooperative partners; and by having an understanding from the outset that although the underlying database would be one entity, the public interfaces would be different.

NOTES

1. Candice M. Benjes and Janis F. Brown. "Database-generated Web Pages: the Norris Medical Library Experience," *Bulletin of the Medical Library Association* 89 no. 2 (2001): 222-224.

2. Michelle Sitko, Narda Tafuri, Gregory Szczyrback, and Taemin Park. "E-journal Management Systems: Trends, Trials, and Trade-offs," *Serials Review* 28 no. 3 (2002): 176-194.

3. Linda A. Rich and Julie L. Rabine. "The Changing Access to Electronic Journals: a Survey of Academic Library Website Revisited," *Serials Review* 27 no. 3/4 (2001): 1-16.

4. Paula D. Watson. "E-journal Management: Acquisition and Control. Special Issue." *Library Technology Reports* 39 no. 2 (2003): 5-72.

5. Adam Chandler and Tim Jewell. A Web Hub for Developing Administrative Metadata for Electronic Resource Management. http://www.library.cornell.edu/cts/elicensestudy/home.html

6. NMLweb site is available at http://www.usc.edu/nml; ISDweb site is available at http://www.usc.edu/isd

7. Bob Boiko. "Understanding Content Management," *Bulletin of the American Society for Information Sciences* 28, no. 1 (Oct/Nov 2001): 8-13.

Integrating and Streamlining Electronic Resources Workflows via Innovative's Electronic Resource Management

Laura Tull
Janet Crum
Trisha Davis
C. Rockelle Strader

SUMMARY. Libraries have been grappling with the management of the growing number of electronic resources, such as e-journals and electronic article indexes, for the last decade especially after the availability of many of these resources on the World Wide Web. The integrated library system wasn't originally designed to accommodate many of these functions. In 2002, Innovative Interfaces, Inc. partnered with several of

Laura Tull is Systems Librarian, Ohio State University Libraries, 1858 Neil Ave Mall, Columbus, OH 43210-1286 (E-mail: tull.9@osu.edu).

Janet Crum is Head, Library Systems and Cataloging, Oregon Health & Science University, PO Box 573, Portland, OR 97207 (E-mail: crumj@ohsu.edu).

Trisha Davis is Head, Serials and Electronic Resources Dept., Ohio State University Libraries, 1858 Neil Ave Mall, Columbus, OH 43210-1286 (E-mail: davis.115@osu.edu).

C. Rockelle Strader is Electronic Resources Manager, Ohio State University Libraries, 1858 Neil Ave Mall, Columbus, OH 43210-1286 (E-mail: strader.2@osu.edu).

[Haworth co-indexing entry note]: "Integrating and Streamlining Electronic Resources Workflows via Innovative's Electronic Resource Management." Tull, Laura et al. Co-published simultaneously in *The Serials Librarian* (The Haworth Information Press, an imprint of The Haworth Press, Inc.) Vol. 47, No. 4, 2005, pp. 103-124; and: *Electronic Journal Management Systems: Experiences from the Field* (ed: Gary Ives) The Haworth Information Press, an imprint of The Haworth Press, Inc., 2005, pp. 103-124. Single or multiple copies of this article are available for a fee from The Haworth Document Delivery Service [1-800-HAWORTH, 9:00 a.m. - 5:00 p.m. (EST). E-mail address: docdelivery@haworthpress.com].

their customer libraries to develop a module to manage electronic resources based on the work of the Digital Library Federation's Electronic Resources Management Initiative. The result of this partnership is a module that addresses functions such as tracking trial access, license negotiations, maintenance, troubleshooting as well as integration into the online catalog. *[Article copies available for a fee from The Haworth Document Delivery Service: 1-800-HAWORTH. E-mail address: <docdelivery@ haworthpress.com> Website: <http://www.HaworthPress.com>* © 2005 by The Haworth Press, Inc. All rights reserved.]

KEYWORDS. Electronic resource management systems, Innovative Interfaces, Inc.

INTRODUCTION

Libraries have struggled to manage the burgeoning number of electronic resources, such as electronic journals and electronic article indexes , especially after many of these resources became available on the World Wide Web. For more than a decade, library staff at Ohio State University (OSU) and the Oregon Health & Science University (OHSU) managed their electronic journals collections by modifying existing systems designed for print journals to fit the descriptive and control needs of the digital format. As collections grew to include thousands of electronic journals and databases, the local adaptations became more complex in nature, more inefficient to use and less effective in describing collections to the library users. Integrated library systems were not originally designed to accommodate many of the functions required for managing these resources, such as licensing, troubleshooting and a public Web display for users. This situation was repeated around the country, leading many research libraries to develop extensive local systems to manage these collections.

LITERATURE REVIEW

By the mid 1990s scholarly articles describing various perspectives on electronic journal publishing were appearing regularly in the library literature. This new format forced changes in workflow for publishers, vendors, acquisitions librarians, serialists, catalogers, preservationists and library Web site designers. Each specialty met significant challenges in adapting policy and processing from the highly standards-driven print format to the wildly varied needs of the electronic format. From the library's perspective overall management seemed impractical during this period of evolution.

The fact that these changes crossed departmental lines further complicated the situation and required more back and forth rather than linear communications within the library, according to Kristin H. Gerhard in her article, "Coordination and Collaboration: Electronic Resources Management."[1] Gerhard clearly stated the need for new models to integrate electronic journals management into library collections and services. Sarah Robbins and Matthew Smith noted that the challenges associated with e-journals management do not simply disappear once access is established and documented in the catalog.[2] Their library at the University of Oklahoma was one of many that developed a local system to manage electronic resources. Robbins and Smith described LORA (Library Online Resource Access) as "one of the most comprehensive and ambitious e-resource management systems currently in use."[3] Yet rather than integrate with the local OPAC, LORA was designed specifically to avoid "the burden of consulting the online catalog, as well as an alphabetical listing of resource titles to see if the library has electronic access to the title they need."[4] Susan Gardner's article "The Impact of Electronic Journals on Library Staff at ARL Member Institutions: A Survey and a Critique of the Survey Methodology"[5] highlights several more locally developed systems. Gardner describes MIT's VERA (Virtual Electronic Resource Access) and notes work done to create a local journal subscription management database at Drexel University.

Another approach to managing electronic journals was described by Gregory Szczyrbak and Louise Pierce of York University of Pennsylvania in a 2002 NASIG workshop.[6] A library task force tested and evaluated three commercially developed electronic serials management systems: Serials Solutions, JournalWebCite, and TDNet. While these systems were designed to track both the library's holdings and the electronic journal holdings in aggregator databases, they initially provided libraries with only holdings lists and usage statistics. More recently such systems have begun to provide additional services such as MARC bibliographic records and URL linking services. They remain an adjunct service to the online catalog and internal acquisitions systems, however. Finally, Elizabeth Meagher and Christopher Brown examined a similar product, Gold Rush, developed by the Colorado Alliance of Research Libraries in their article "Gold Rush: Integrated Access to Aggregated Journal Text through the OPAC."[7] Gold Rush can link to the 856 MARC field in serial records and offers "subscription tracking and notification services, which assist serials acquisitions units."[8] Yet, even this well designed, highly functional system operates as a partner to the local library system rather than as an integral function.

DEVELOPMENT OF AN INTEGRATED ELECTRONIC RESOURCE MANAGEMENT MODULE

In 2000, the Digital Library Federation (DLF) commissioned three reports concerning digital collections. A report by Timothy Jewell of the University of

Washington Libraries (UWL) surveyed the management practices of several large research libraries concerning their licensed commercial electronic resources.[9] The report, entitled *Selection and Presentation of Commercially Available Electronic Resources: Issues and Practices*, reveals that many of these libraries developed local systems to support the multitude of tasks required to manage these resources. After the report was published, the Electronic Resources Management Initiative (ERMI), sponsored by the DLF, began developing specifications and tools for managing these resources. In 2002, the DLF sponsored a workshop with the National Information Standards Organization (NISO) to examine the need for standards in this area. Jewell and Adam Chandler of the Cornell University Library maintain a Web hub that records the work of the ERMI and highlights developments in the general arena of electronic resource management.[10] It includes documentation associated with the deliverables of the ERMI including workflow, functional requirements, entity relationship diagram, system data structure and data element dictionary. The submission drafts were sent to the DLF for prepublication editing in July 2004, and are available via the Web hub, while editing takes place. Once the final report is published, NISO and the DLF will discuss the next steps in the standards process.

In 2002, administration at UWL began discussions with their library system vendor, Innovative Interfaces, Inc., about the functional requirements for an electronic resource management module. They formed a development partnership, and Innovative installed a prototype of a staff module at UWL in the fall of 2002. Glasgow University, Ohio State University, the University of Western Australia and Washington State University joined the development partnership that fall. Other libraries, including Oregon Health & Science University Library, assisted during the beta test phase of the product. The goal of the partnership was to develop a module, based on the work of the DLF ERMI, to manage electronic resources. This module would be integrated into Innovative's Millennium library system. Grover and Fons describe these goals in more detail: "Some of these goals included integrating licensing and purchasing details using a single interface, streamlining workflows, eliminating the need to maintain separate spreadsheets and databases, and storing and selectively displaying information in the online catalog for staff and patrons."[11] The product is simply called Electronic Resource Management (ERM).

This article describes how OSU and OHSU applied ERM to support selection, licensing, purchase, maintenance, user support, and public access tasks. The resulting applications interface smoothly with existing systems and workflows and remain virtually transparent to the user. The following sections outline a typical electronic resource management workflow with details about how ERM provides specific functions and fields in each record to support each step in the process. As development progressed, Innovative also developed a stand-alone version of the module for libraries without Millennium. Utah State University, Cornell University, and the Library of Congress have purchased the stand-alone product. All sections in this article are relevant to the stand-alone product except those that describe ERM's integration with the on-line catalog and reporting tools.

RECORD STRUCTURE

Innovative developed three new types of records for managing electronic resources: resource, license and contact (see Figures 1, 2 and 3). The resource record describes the resource providing public information fields such as coverage, resource URL, and description as well as fields for staff to manage the resource such as access information, usage statistics, user support, and an incident log for troubleshooting. The license record provides contractual details with fields such as site definition, authorized users, authentication method and terms of use. The contact record contains details about any organization or company involved in providing access to an electronic resource.

As with using any new system, libraries will have to define how they will use these records in conjunction with their current workflow. This includes defining which fields to use as well as understanding what information to include

FIGURE 1. Resource record.

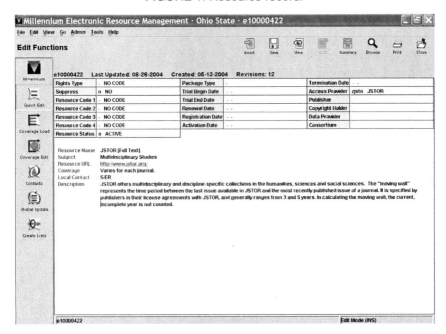

FIGURE 2. License record.

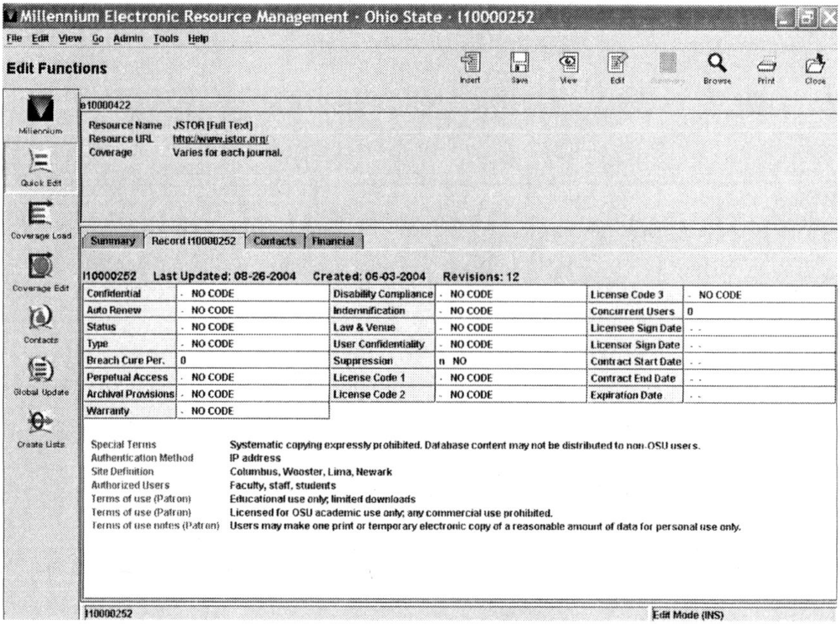

in each field. The design of resource and license records includes a mix of fixed- and variable-length fields similar to that of MARC-formatted bibliographic records. These provide the necessary flexibility for recording and handling the complex details of managing electronic resources. Libraries define coded values for fixed-length fields, as they can for other records in Millennium. Libraries can also customize fields in the record by renaming them or adding new ones. Innovative can add multiple labeled lines to any variable-length field for better organization of information within that field. For example the incident log field has 5 lines labeled as follows: incident, date/time, reported by, reported to, follow-up action. Libraries can also request Innovative to make multivalue variable-length fields to be able to specify a pick list of values so that staff can select information quickly and consistently. Unlike coded data in fixed-length fields, staff can also enter free text not on the pick list if necessary.

SELECTION

The selection of electronic resources, both databases and electronic journals, at the most basic level is not unlike that of traditional print resources. Li-

FIGURE 3. Contact record.

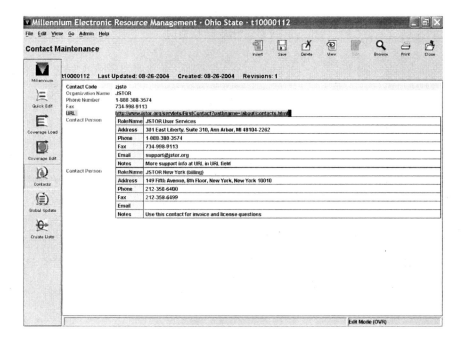

brarians evaluate titles under consideration in terms of their content: Do they support an institution's curriculum or a library's program? Is the content reliable? However, there are further issues that need to be addressed when considering electronic formats:

- Does the electronic resource provide access to material that is not available in another format?
- Does the electronic resource provide access more effectively than other forms of access to this information?
- Is the electronic access worth the cost?
- Is the electronic resource stable?
- If the resource is a database, does it provide full-text articles or links to full text?
- If the resource is an electronic journal, what is the range of holdings? Are backfiles included with current issue access, or are they accessed separately? Does the title come bundled with print, or is it available online only?
- Will the library have rights to perpetual access to content for the years for which a subscription was held?

- Is the resource part of a larger package containing several titles?
- Is the title available through more than one provider? Is there a preference?
- Is the resource compatible with browsers and operating systems used by the library?

In many cases, trial access to the resource can be established that can answer many of these questions. However, trial versions, usually restricted by password, may allow access to only part of the content. Issues such as access via IP addresses and proxy servers for remote access must be dealt with separately but are crucial to the selection process.

Many libraries keep most, if not all, information gathered from trials in separate documents and spreadsheets, but ERM provides a method to consolidate this information, making it readily available to staff who manage the selection and acquisition process for electronic resources. The resource record stores most of the necessary information for tracking selection. Content and basic selection criteria may be recorded in description and note fields. The coverage field provides information about the dates of coverage, such as "1997 to present." The access information field is also pertinent to selection, providing details regarding, for example, IP, proxy or remote access. Trial information is a discrete field that can include a summary of findings or an active link to a more substantial document or Web site. Coded data, including dates such as trial beginning and end dates, are recorded in fixed-length fields. Information such as resource and package types, which tend to be limited in scope and easily defined, may also be set up with customizable codes.

An enthusiastically received feature of ERM is the resource management tickler. Its usefulness is pervasive throughout ERM, from tracking the ends of trials to monitoring the status of licenses and invoices in addition to receiving renewal reminders. This tool for tracking and follow-up relies upon date fields in the resource and license records to send e-mail reminders. It can be set up in two ways: It can be set to automatically scan resource or license records according to customizable parameters; or, a tickler message can be entered manually to send a single e-mail at a particular time. In either case, once a message has been sent, the system generates an entry in a tickler log that is placed in the flagged resource or license record.

Libraries can choose to retain records for trials that do not result in purchase as a record of their evaluation, in case that resource is recommended for purchase again in the future.

LICENSING

In a 2001 NASIG workshop presented by Jill Emery and Renulfo Ramirez, Gail Teaster reported that "Maintaining paper files of licenses and responding to questions and problems related to licensing agreements can become over-whelming."[12] The care and maintenance of fully executed license agreements and the tracking of their terms have been a challenge to libraries for more than a decade. In practical terms, libraries have coped by storing licensing information in paper files, in notes in local online records, or developing local systems to handle the data. At the University of Florida Libraries, licenses were scanned, stored as PDF files, and linked directly to the title in the online catalog for staff and patron use.[13] At MIT, a sophisticated system named VERA provides license details combined with holdings notes, product description, access locations, order information and a URL link to the scanned license.[14]

The ERM license record, however, provides a single place for storing license terms, rights management data, detailed contractual information, and if desired, a link to a digital copy of the license itself. At OSU, the license record is used primarily for coding licensed rights and storing contractual details for licensed databases. Once a license agreement is fully executed and access to the product is confirmed, the license terms are used for three purposes: to alert library staff to the product's rights and restrictions, to alert users to use rights and restrictions, and to resolve suspected breaches. The key benefit of the license record is that staff from any library department have a single centralized online source for all their information needs regarding the license terms. Staff can quickly retrieve data traditionally stored in notes in order records or in lists and spreadsheets in various departments.

The license record is attached to an established resource record and information from the license record can display in the online catalog in both the resource record and any linked bibliographic records. Details about the online catalog are in the user support section. Anyone familiar with Millennium will understand the license record's structure and navigation immediately. As with the resource record, the library simply needs to decide which fields will be most useful for their own workflow and to define values for specific fixed- and variable-length fields.

Figure 2 shows the two sections of a license record. The first section contains fixed-length fields that provide information about the type of product, and contractual terms such as start and end dates for access. Some libraries will review the license and enter the contractual terms into fields such as indemnification, cure period for breach, and confidentiality clauses. The second section provides variable-length fields to delineate details regarding access and archival rights. Library staff can enter rights pertaining to interlibrary loan, course packs, and electronic reserves in the terms of use (staff) field. End user rights are stored in the terms of use (patron) field. These fields allow the library to spell out the permitted and restricted uses for the resource. Multivalue fields have proved quite useful for several license fields. OSU Libraries requested this type of field for site definition, authorized users, terms of use and local subjects. For example, OSU has several campuses across the state. Sometimes the license only permits the Columbus campus to use a resource. The site definition field was set to include a list of values such as "All OSU"; "Columbus, Wooster"; "Columbus, Wooster, Lima, Newark"; etc. When staff insert this field into the record, they pick a value from a pop-up list and can also add free-text information if necessary.

PURCHASE

Managing the purchase of electronic resources is a process with three primary facets: pricing; initial set-up and confirmation of access; and renewal and cancellation. Pricing involves documenting such information as discounts and consortial participation. The initial set-up includes recording URLs, activation dates, and contact information. Renewal and cancellation involves documenting and tracking renewal dates and changes in the status of a title.

Pricing models vary. If the resource is an electronic journal, it may come free with print, it may be purchased for a fee in addition to print, or it may be electronic only. The purchased format must be clearly documented. Consortial deals, multiple-title pricing, and discounts must also be recorded. Prices and fees themselves, as well as to whom payment is made, are recorded in the order record for each product or package. The resource record contains designated fields for information specific to electronic resources such as package type, pricing and payment, and consortium.

ERM provides linking of order records to resource records. An order record may first be attached to a bibliographic record and then linked to a resource record, or an order record may be directly attached to a resource record without an associated bibliographic record. The latter option may be particularly useful for managing multiple-title packages which are paid on one invoice or for which there is a single license. ERM also allows flexibility in determining the most appropriate place to store specific types of information. Notes regarding pricing and discounts that may have been awkwardly placed in order records or in separate documents may now be consolidated in the resource record. The initial set-up for a purchased resource includes recording access URLs, contact information, and activation dates. While some contact information may be provided in a trial (if a trial was done), the access URLs used in the final purchased product are often different from those used in trials, and activation and registration dates are usually tied to the purchase itself.

Several organizations or companies may be involved when purchasing an electronic resource. Some titles are purchased directly from a publisher or access provider, while others are brokered through subscription agents or other third-party vendors. The entity that receives the actual payment is recorded in the order record, but since this could be a third party, it is necessary to separately record publisher and/or provider information. In many cases, once access is established, the access provider or publisher, not the agent to whom payment was rendered, may be the primary contact for troubleshooting problems. Within each company there may be different contacts for account support, technical support, etc.

Staff enter these company details in the contact record. It contains fields for general information about a company plus a repeatable field to enter information about specific individuals at a company designated as the library's contacts. Once staff create a contact record, they can link to it from fields in the resource record for access provider, publisher, copyright holder, and data provider. Staff can view the contact record from the resource record and find the appropriate person with whom to communicate.

Since most resources are licensed on a subscription basis, it becomes imperative to track renewal dates and related issues such as price changes and provider changes. Registration, activation, renewal, and termination dates have specific fields in the resource record. The resource record also provides fields for staff notes, administration notes, and pricing/payment notes that are more appropriately associated with the resource itself than with the financial aspects that are tracked in the order record. As noted in the discussion on selection, the resource management tickler is particularly useful for sending reminders, such as when a resource's expiration date looms near.

LOADING AND MANAGING ELECTRONIC HOLDINGS

Once a resource has been purchased and activated, the library must decide how to manage it. For electronic journals in particular, these decisions can be challenging. Should these titles be entered in the catalog? Should they be appended to the catalog record for the print version or cataloged with separate records? If separate records are used, should they be brief or full records? How can holdings from large full-text databases be maintained in the catalog when there are so many of them, and they change so frequently? ERM addresses these questions by enabling libraries to create holdings records and link them to bibliographic records by batch-loading a text file of holdings data. It also enables links between holdings records and their parent resource records. The result of this two-way link is that information can be presented in the online catalog in a unique way, which is described in more detail in the user support section. This section will explore the steps involved in loading and managing electronic holdings: obtaining holdings data, loading it into ERM initially, maintaining and updating the data, and integrating ERM with other systems that use electronic holdings.

Loading Holdings

The first step in loading electronic holdings is to get accurate, complete holdings data in a format that ERM can load. Libraries can obtain this data from a third-party provider such as Serials Solutions (*http://www.serialssolutions.com*),

TDNet (*http://www.tdnet.com*) or EBSCO A to Z (*http://www.ebsco.com/ atoz*), all of which offer a file format compatible with ERM. Libraries that already subscribe to one of these services should have little difficulty obtaining a data file to load. Libraries that do not subscribe to one of these services will need to decide whether to do so or use a homegrown system to generate the data. Some issues to consider when making this decision include how difficult it will be to generate a compatible file from a homegrown system versus how much effort will be required to implement a vendor-supplied service, and whether the effort saved is worth the cost of the service. OHSU library staff decided to use their local electronic journal database–which contained nearly all the necessary information–along with title lists supplied by vendors of full-text databases. Submitting all of OHSU's local data to a vendor's service proved to be nearly as much effort as adapting the local database to suit ERM; hence it seemed more straightforward to use the local system. Libraries that subscribe to many full-text databases, however, may be better off with a vendor.

Once the library has obtained accurate holdings data in a compatible format, these holdings can be loaded into ERM using the Coverage Load feature. Coverage load performs the following tasks:

- Loads holdings data into the Coverage Database, a relational database containing the provider name, ISSN, title, starting and ending dates of coverage, URL, and the following optional fields: ISSN for the electronic version (EISSN), embargo period, ISBN, holdings, and four user-defined fields
- Creates Innovative holdings records, including MARC holdings if desired
- Links holdings records to bibliographic records based on the incoming ISSN and title. If no matching bibliographic record is found, Coverage Load can create brief records with user-specified parameters
- Links holdings records to resource records, thereby connecting the holdings with information about the parent resource

As part of the loading process, library staff need to decide how electronic journals will be cataloged. ERM is designed to attach incoming holdings to existing bibliographic records when possible. Library staff can specify whether or not brief bibliographic records should be created when a matching bibliographic record is not found and can also specify fixed- and variable-length field data to be inserted in those brief records. ERM allows users to load titles from a single provider, even when all holdings are combined in a single, large file, allowing cataloging decisions to be made on a provider-by-provider basis.

Maintaining and Updating Holdings

Once holdings have been loaded into the system, they must be updated regularly. In addition to the title changes serials librarians love to hate, electronic resources are notorious for other types of changes–new URLs, changes in dates of coverage, changes in embargo periods, etc. These changes must be documented quickly to avoid a slew of complaints from irritated users who cannot access their favorite journals. Each library must decide how coverage data will be updated–with files from a vendor such as Serials Solutions, title lists from database vendors, and/or manual updates, title by title. ERM can be used with any combination of these options.

ERM provides two means for updating coverage information–batch loading and individual changes. New files of coverage data may be loaded with Coverage Load, using the same process described above. Libraries that obtain holdings data from commercial services can therefore update their coverage data by simply loading the new file. When the load is complete, ERM reports on new records created and existing records updated, as well as existing records not updated (see Figure 4). The latter can be investigated and deleted if access is no longer available. Coverage can also be updated manually using ERM's Coverage Edit mode (see Figure 5). This feature is useful for updating small numbers of titles and allows libraries to keep holdings information current. One cannot, however, add new holdings through Coverage Edit; new holdings can only be added from a file via Coverage Load. The ability to add holdings manually is planned for a future release.

Integrating Holdings with Other Systems

Many library systems use electronic holdings data. Databases such as Ovid, PubMed, and ISI Web of Knowledge allow libraries to load holdings so that

FIGURE 4. Results of coverage load.

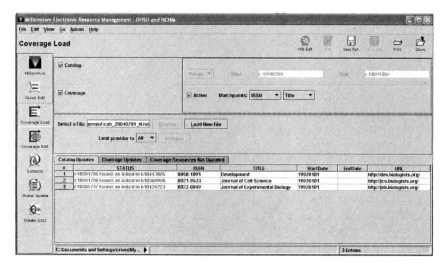

FIGURE 5. Coverage edit.

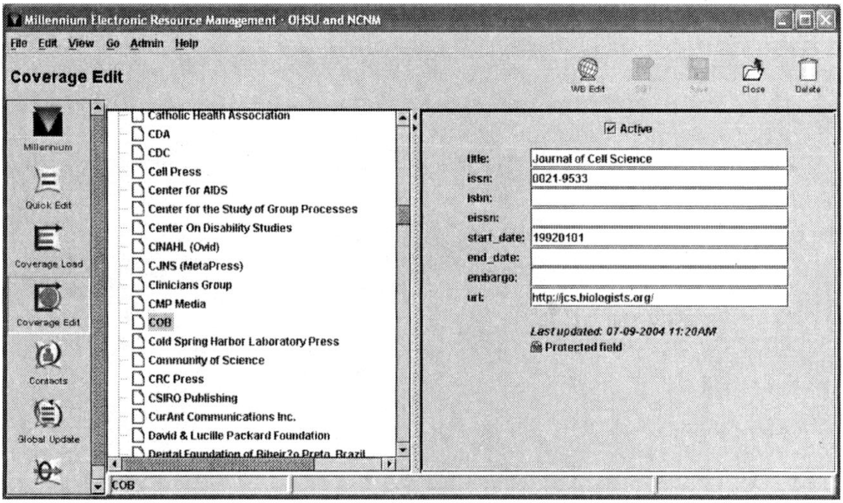

users can limit searches to full text and/or link directly to article text from a citation. OpenURL resolvers rely on electronic holdings data to determine whether or not to offer links to full text. And, many libraries maintain Web-based lists or databases of electronic journal holdings for patron use. Maintaining holdings data manually in all these places is wasteful duplication of effort; holdings should be maintained in one place and output to other systems automatically whenever possible. Library staff implementing ERM need to determine where ERM will fit in the scheme of systems that use electronic holdings data. Will ERM be one of many systems that receive holdings data that originates somewhere else, or will holdings be maintained in ERM and sent to other systems? Some libraries will maintain all their holdings data through a vendor such as Serials Solutions, then use the data from that vendor to populate ERM and other systems. Others may choose to maintain holdings data in an in-house database and use it as their central data source. Staff at the OHSU hope to use ERM as the central source for holdings data, once Innovative adds the ability to export the coverage database to a flat file. Then, corrections to holdings data will be immediately available in the catalog.

REPORTING

At some point, library staff will also need to get data out of ERM to create statistical reports, answer survey questions, generate title lists, etc. Data can be output from ERM using Create Lists, Innovative's reporting tool. With this tool, libraries can generate lists of records with specified values in specified fields, then output fields from these records in delimited text files. For example, a library could generate a list of all holdings records created in a given month, then output the titles to create a list of new journal subscriptions. Create Lists also works with other ERM record types, allowing libraries to output data from resource and license records. Unfortunately, Create Lists does not allow clean output of the start date and end date of holdings, which makes this tool somewhat less useful. In a future release, Innovative plans to allow users to output the entire coverage database as a flat file. Currently, Innovative does not support direct SQL queries to the Coverage Database.

Libraries that have Millennium have access to Millennium Statistics, statistical reporting tools that generate aggregated data, cross tab analyses, etc. With Release 2005, libraries that have purchased the stand-alone ERM product will also have Millennium Statistics.

Libraries implementing ERM should consider the tradeoff between reporting and maintenance. Adding additional fields to records, such as the MARC 008 in holdings records, allows for more powerful reporting capabilities, but this data must be entered accurately and kept current, which often requires considerable maintenance time. Libraries with Millennium can use batch processing tools such as Rapid Update to facilitate maintenance, but time and thought are still required to maintain accurate data. OHSU Library staff are currently considering these issues and will likely create richer data for some holdings (e.g., those for which the library has acquired permanent access rights) than for other, more ephemeral holdings.

USER SUPPORT

Web Presentation

From the beginning of the development partnership with Innovative, presentation of electronic resources in the online catalog was integral to the project. Information from the resource and license records would display in the online catalog in a similar manner to bibliographic records. Innovative developed the staff module first, followed by the online catalog display. The resource name and subject indexes may be searched in the online catalog alongside traditional indexes such as author, title, and subject. The resource record display includes fields from resource records and their attached license records (see Figure 6).

The library defines which fields display to the public. Fields in the resource record such as description, coverage dates, resource URL, public notes and user support provide information, connect the user to the resource and help the user understand how to use it. Some fields in the resource and license records

FIGURE 6. Resource record display in the online catalog with license information in table.

Note the resource advisory note and linked holdings to journals in JSTOR below the license information.

can contain URLs that will display to the public as hyperlinks. For example, staff could enter hyperlinks in the description field to link to detailed documentation on the library's or a vendor's Web site about an electronic resource. Several fields in the license record are also well-suited for public display, i.e., site definition, authorized users, number of concurrent users, and terms of use. While some libraries with locally developed systems have been able to provide some license information to users, in many libraries this information is still in paper form, locked away in file cabinets. Making some of this information available in the online catalog can help public services staff and users understand how a resource may be accessed and used. Publicizing terms of use in this way also enables libraries to comply with license clauses that require them to notify users of prohibited uses. Libraries can specify field labels for the online catalog that are understandable to users. For example, at the OSU Libraries, the public display label for the site definition field in the license record is "Authorized locations," while the public display label for the terms of use (patron) field in the license record is labeled "Permitted uses."

As noted in the section on loading holdings, when coverage data is loaded, ERM can link a holdings record to both the bibliographic and resource records. These links enable an attractive, informative online catalog display. A list of all linked electronic journal titles and their holdings will display at the end of the resource record. Fields from the license record will display not only in the parent resource record but on all of the individual bibliographic records for linked journals. The same is true of information in the resource advisory field in a resource record, which is used to communicate temporary problems for a particular resource (see Figure 7).

When a user views a bibliographic record, all holdings loaded through ERM are displayed in a table near the top of the screen. The library can customize the display of the information in the bibliographic record to include not only the holdings information but also a link to the resource, and a link to the record for the resource. URLs for electronic journals can be entered in the holdings record instead of the bibliographic record, which provides different display options (see Figure 8).

FIGURE 7. Bibliographic record display at OSU for an electronic journal in JSTOR.

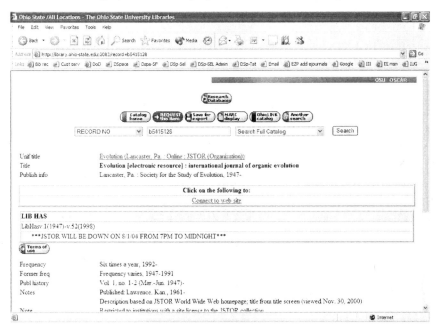

Note the resource advisory note display and link to license information through the terms of use button.

FIGURE 8. Bibliographic record display at OHSU.

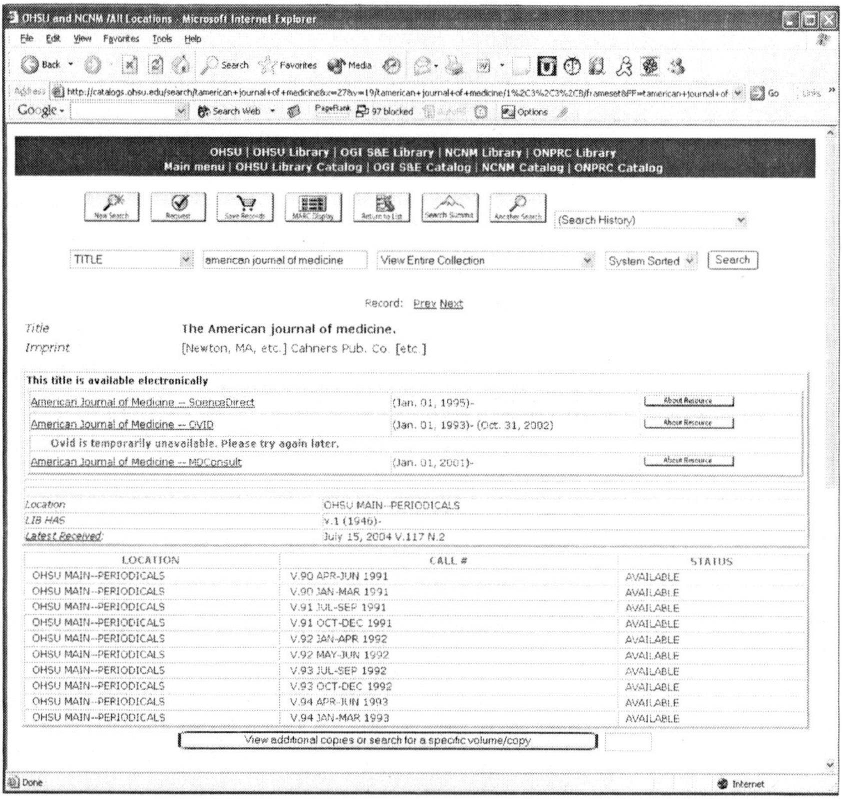

When electronic resources became available on the Web, many libraries organized their Web sites to help users find appropriate resources for their research. Although many libraries catalog their electronic resources to make them available in the online catalog, some libraries have also provided separate sections on their Web sites for electronic resources such as article index databases or electronic journals to help users quickly find the appropriate resource for their needs. At first, these resources were organized with static Web pages, which proved to be time-consuming to maintain. If the URL for a particular resource changed, the URL had to be located and changed on every page that referenced it. Dynamic Web pages eased the maintenance burden by using a variety of open source and commercial databases to store information in one location for display on multiple Web pages. Scripts, embedded in the HTML code, pulled information from the database to display on Web pages.

Libraries could also use software to create Web interfaces for staff members to input records into the database without learning HTML or FTP.

Some of the development partners and beta testers wanted to list resources separately on their Web sites as they do now, as well as have them integrated into the online catalog. ERM can accommodate both options. Many of the research libraries mentioned in Jewell's report and listed on the Web hub had developed similar ways of presenting lists of electronic resources on their Web sites. These include browsable lists of titles by letter of the alphabet, lists by subject and the ability to search for a resource by name or keyword. Innovative's highly customizable online catalog allows customers to easily create local Web pages that link into the online catalog. Two elements of ERM are key to reproducing this functionality. The first one, the resource name index, indexes the resource name field in the resource record. Innovative provided this field and its accompanying index with the staff module so this was already in place when Innovative staff began to work on the online catalog display. This index provides the basis for a browsable list of resources by letter of the alphabet as well as a search box to search by name. Innovative provided the second index, a local resource subject index, during development of the online catalog display to enable libraries to list their electronic resources by local subjects. The regular subject indexes that use Library of Congress Subject Headings and Medical Subject Headings work within the context of bibliographic records, but many libraries prefer simpler, very broad subject categories to guide users to appropriate electronic resources. With both indexes in place, it is easy to provide links on a Web page by constructing URLs that search the index for all the resources that begin with a particular letter or have a particular local subject (see Figure 9). Clicking the link returns a browse display from the online catalog. ERM acts as the backend for pages that retain the look and feel of Web pages from previous systems.

Troubleshooting

Electronic resources suffer from many problems unique to the electronic format. Personal computers, Web browsers, and networks all produce a number of variables that can interfere with the proper functioning of an electronic resource. Another layer of complexity is added by proxy servers, used to provide access to electronic resources from locations outside the campus network.

The inability to connect to a particular electronic resource is one of the most common problems reported to public services staff. Generally, problems with resources can be placed into one of two broad categories: technology-based (e.g., server problems, software glitches, misunderstanding of the resource's properties and functions, etc.) or subscription-based (e.g., license or renewal issues, which have been discussed in other parts of this article). Technology-based problems affect users most often. After troubleshooting the local vari-

FIGURE 9. OSU's gateway page to electronic resources.

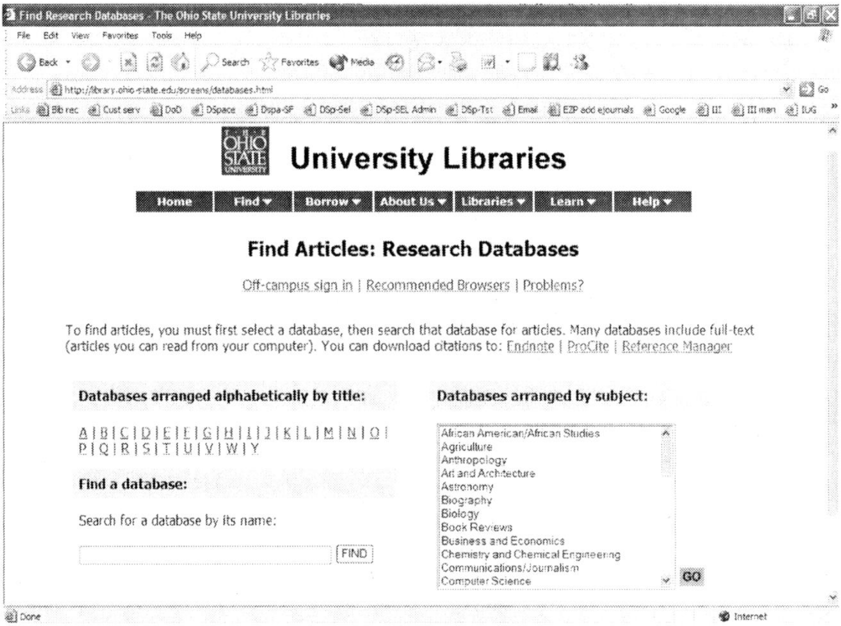

ables that could interfere with connections, the problem can usually be narrowed down to the resource itself. Common problems are that a server is down at the provider's site or that the resource does not work with some types of software, such as a particular Web browser or operating system. Other common problems are that users do not know how to perform specific functions within an electronic resource, or a function that used to work no longer does, including printing, e-mailing and downloading records, or displaying an article in a particular format, such as PDF.

ERM has several fields to assist with tracking access problems in a variety of ways. If a problem requires communication with the provider, staff can display contact information from the contact record to find the phone number for technical support, for example. The resource record also contains an incident log, a field to record the nature of the problem, date and time, who reported the problem, who was contacted, and follow-up notes. If necessary, staff can set the resource management tickler in the resource record, and the system will send an e-mail reminder to follow up with the provider on a particular date.

ERM provides a method to communicate problems of short- and long-term duration to public services staff and users via the online catalog. For example, if a provider's server goes down for scheduled maintenance or because of technical problems, staff can enter a resource advisory note in the resource record. This field displays prominently in the online catalog in the resource record as well as in any of the records linked to that resource (see Figures 6 and 7). Users and public services staff will see there is a problem whether they display the parent resource record to search an article index, for example, or they go directly to one of the electronic journals within that article index. Staff can enter problems of a more permanent nature, such as when a resource will not work with particular kinds of software, in public note fields in the resource record. Note that these will display in the resource record but not in the linked records.

CONCLUSION

Innovative is the first vendor to integrate electronic resource management into their library system. ERM addresses many aspects of electronic resources that were difficult to manage within the existing library system structure. Specifically, it addresses issues with selection and acquisitions such as tracking trial databases, and license negotiations, as well as troubleshooting. The Coverage Load function eases the maintenance of electronic journals within aggregator databases, establishing a link between the parent resource and the journals. For libraries that use Millennium, ERM integrates electronic resources into the library management system to a degree not previously possible. Electronic resources are completely integrated into the online catalog, reporting tools and Innovative's OpenURL resolver, WebBridge. WebBridge shares the ERM Coverage Database, allowing libraries to update holdings simultaneously for both products.

The complex nature of managing electronic resources has been addressed by the Digital Library Federation's Electronic Resource Management Initiative. Their work may provide the basis for new standards in this area, which will likely encourage development of standard data models and workflow for electronic resources. Although libraries that have developed local systems may continue to enhance those systems for the present, it will be interesting to see if they will be maintained when other library system vendors release electronic resource management products. VTLS and Endeavor, among others, have closely followed the DLF ERMI and are developing their own products to fill this need.

NOTES

1. Kristin H. Gerhard. "Coordination and Collaboration: A Model for Electronic Resources Management" in *E-Serials: Publishers, Libraries, Users, and Standards*, 2nd ed., ed. Wayne Jones (Binghamton, NY: Haworth Press, 2003), 111-118.
2. Sarah Robbins and Matthew Smith. "Managing E-Resources: a Database-Driven Approach" in *E-Serials Collection Management: Transitions, Trends, and*

Technicalities, ed. David C. Fowler (Binghamton, NY: Haworth Press, 2004), 239-251.

3. Ibid., 240.

4. Ibid., 251.

5. Susan Gardner. "The Impact of Electronic Journals on Library Staff at ARL Member Institutions: a Survey and a Critique of the Survey Methodology," *Serials Review*, 27, no. 3/4 (2001): 17-32.

6. Karen Mathews. "E-Journal Subscription Management Systems and Beyond," *The Serials Librarian*, 44, no. 3/4 (2003): 157-162.

7. Elizabeth S. Meagher and Christopher C. Brown. "Gold Rush: Integrated Access to Aggregated Journal Text Through the OPAC," *Library Resources and Technical Services*, 48, no. 1 (2004): 69-76.

8. Ibid., 74.

9. Timothy D. Jewell. *Selection and Presentation of Commercially Available Electronic Resources: Issues and Practices* (Washington, DC: Digital Library Federation, Council on Library and Information Resources, 2001).

10. Adam Chandler and Tim Jewell. A Web Hub for Developing Administrative Metadata for Electronic Resource Management. Updated 2004-03-15. *http://www.library.cornell.edu/cts/elicensestudy/home.html* (accessed June 22, 2004).

11. Diane Grover and Theodore Fons. "The Innovative Electronic Resource Management System: A Development Partnership," *Serials Review* 30, no. 2 (Summer 2004): 111-112.

12. Gale Teaster. "Tackling the Monolith: Licensing Management at the Consortial and Local Levels," *The Serials Librarian*, 42, no. 3/4 (2002): 275-280.

13. Marie R. Kennedy, Michele J. Crump, and Douglas Kiker. "Paper to PDF: Making License Agreements Accessible Through the OPAC," *Library Resources and Technical Services*, 48, no. 1 (2004): 20-25.

14. Ellen Finnie Duranceau. "License Tracking," *The Serials Librarian*, 26, no. 3 (2000): 69-73.

Electronic Resources Management Systems: The Experience of Beta Testing and Implementation

Tony A. Harvell

SUMMARY. The management of electronic resources is one of the most challenging issues facing academic libraries today. Integrated library systems are often unable to manage these resources using existing architecture, but many vendors and individuals are developing systems as either stand-alone or components of their integrated library systems. This paper outlines the investigation, evaluation and implementation process of one library that served as a beta test library with an integrated library system vendor to develop an electronic resource management system. The challenge of developing standards that address both interoperability and diverse libraries and resource types is highlighted. *[Article copies available for a fee from The Haworth Document Delivery Service: 1-800-HAWORTH. E-mail address: <docdelivery@haworthpress.com> Website: <http://www.HaworthPress.com> © 2005 by The Haworth Press, Inc. All rights reserved.]*

Tony A. Harvell is Head of Acquisitions, University of California San Diego Libraries, 9500 Gilman Drive 0175-A, LaJolla, CA 92093-0175 (E-mail: tharvell@ucsd.edu).

[Haworth co-indexing entry note]: "Electronic Resources Management Systems: The Experience of Beta Testing and Implementation." Harvell, Tony A. Co-published simultaneously in *The Serials Librarian* (The Haworth Information Press, an imprint of The Haworth Press, Inc.) Vol. 47, No. 4, 2005, pp. 125-136; and: *Electronic Journal Management Systems: Experiences from the Field* (ed: Gary Ives) The Haworth Information Press, an imprint of The Haworth Press, Inc., 2005, pp. 125-136. Single or multiple copies of this article are available for a fee from The Haworth Document Delivery Service [1-800-HAWORTH, 9:00 a.m. - 5:00 p.m. (EST). E-mail address: docdelivery@haworthpress.com].

KEYWORDS. Electronic resources management, beta testing, standards, interoperability, ERMS

OVERVIEW OF ISSUE

Managing electronic resources is one of the most complex challenges facing academic libraries these days. The workflows for acquiring these resources along with the need to incorporate bibliographic, financial, and rights management information is generally not supported by existing integrated library systems. The life cycle of electronic resources is quite different from that of print resources since it is characterized by activities such as trials and license and business terms negotiation as well as an ongoing review process. The functional responsibilities for managing electronic resources are often distributed over several library departments (e.g., serials, acquisitions, library systems, legal counsel, and collection development). As licensing electronic resources has greatly increased in recent years, libraries have struggled to control this information in a variety of ways: paper files, integrated library systems, separate databases stored on local computers or networked, and locally developed systems designed to be distributed to a variety of library users. The information stored in electronic resources management systems often has great relevance to public service operations–delivering holdings and access information to users along with license permissions and restrictions to both library staff and public users.

Most, but not all, electronic resources are serial in nature. For some time, most libraries have been struggling to track both print and electronic access within existing serials control systems. When most electronic journal access was "free with print," it did not require the close monitoring of electronic access and subscription payment. However, as electronic access became a premium service for electronic journals, libraries felt compelled to more closely monitor these resources and carefully review licensing information. In the early days of e-journal access, most agreements were click-through licenses that were often not closely scrutinized by many libraries. With the shift in the subscription pricing model to online rather than print (i.e., "flipped") libraries were required to devote even more attention to both the business and license terms of their agreements, particularly when pricing and cancellation restrictions were in effect. In addition, the proliferation of access providers including vendor (e.g., ScienceDirect) and third-party based (Ingenta, Highwire) and potential overlap with aggregator content required libraries to have much better control of electronic resources.

BACKGROUND INFORMATION ON THE LIBRARY

The University of California, San Diego (UCSD) Libraries subscribe to a large number of electronic resources in an environment that includes nine branch libraries. In general, technical services (including acquisitions and licensing of electronic resources) is centralized. In addition to locally licensed resources, UCSD libraries also have access to a large number of resources licensed and acquired through the California Digital Library (CDL). CDL is a "co-library" of the University of California and has as part of its mission ". . . investing in the means of developing, acquiring access to, and persistently managing digital collections."[1] Using a variety of formulas, individual campuses obtain access to electronic journals and other electronic resources through the CDL Shared Collections Program. In the past, many electronic resources had been centrally purchased and locally loaded into MELVYL (a union catalog of the University of California Libraries). With the move to a more distributed model using the vendor's platform and native interface in 2000, individual libraries took on a greater role in selecting the interface and determining their level of participation in purchasing at the campus level.

UCSD Libraries had begun licensing resources locally in the early 1990s and had developed extensive paper files with license and business information. In addition, the bibliographic and acquisitions information (order and payment information) was being tracked in the Libraries' Innovative Interfaces integrated library system. As electronic resources proliferated in number, more bibliographers wanted to arrange trials and the volume of communication with vendors was increasing. It was becoming increasingly difficult to ensure that all library staff had adequate access to where a resource was in the workflow and to relevant licensing information that was related to access and resource availability. Though the purchasing and licensing was being done through the Acquisitions Department, the Catalog Department has the responsibility to provide access through the OPAC and needed all relevant information on the available content and licensing restrictions that needed to be reflected in the catalog record. The Acquisitions Department staff would also provide the Catalog Department information on the mode of access, IP address, simultaneous use restrictions and other relevant information. This had been handled through e-mail messages sent back and forth, not making for the most efficient communication in a systematic and timely fashion. Occasionally, the catalogers needed to contact the vendor's technical support staff to identify a precise URL to make links at the title level. As UCSD Libraries acquired more resources and deeper backfiles, this activity became more cumbersome.

IDENTIFYING THE FUNCTIONAL NEEDS FOR MANAGING ELECTRONIC RESOURCES

It became clear that something was needed that would allow us to manage electronic resources in a more systematic way. Because the activity related to electronic resources was quite decentralized, we began to identify the functional needs of each area that worked with electronic resources.

From an acquisitions standpoint, electronic resources management required far more follow-up than print acquisitions. While the integrated library system allowed us to claim print publications systematically, we had no mechanism to alert us when activities related to licensing electronic resources needed to be prompted (e.g., follow-up on signing a license, advance notification before cancellation, access follow-up, etc.). Both technical services and public services staff have had the unpleasant experience of dealing with an unhappy patron when a resource is unavailable. This experience is made even more unpleasant when it is the result of the library not following up on the licensing or payment process only to have the electronic access suddenly terminated.

From a bibliographic standpoint, it also became increasingly difficult to reflect the relationships between individual journal titles and electronic resources of e-journal packages. This was particularly true of journal titles that are available from more than one provider (e.g., *Journal of the History of Ideas* is available from LION, Project Muse, and JSTOR). The traditional MARC fields for linking (usually 710s, 730s, and 790s) did not accomplish this very well from an acquisitions standpoint. As the libraries' collection budget became leaner, it was imperative to be able to identify duplicate coverage in electronic resources as easily as we do in print resources.

In many cases, the pricing of the print counterpart was tied to the electronic and vice versa. It was often difficult to express those financial relationships within the confines of existing order and payment records in the system.

From a licensing standpoint, we needed to be able to track and communicate relevant license information easily to our Interlibrary Loan staff as well as public users. Most electronic resources vendors or publishers have either a stated or implied obligation on the part of the library to communicate relevant license terms to our users. Our library had been scanning redacted licenses in PDF and mounting them within the library Web site. However, this information was not easily located by our users, and the interlibrary loan staff often had difficulty identifying the relevant sections or understanding what the restrictions were. We needed some way to make the most essential licensing terms available to both staff and users in an easy and readable way. We also needed to have a grasp on the different types of contractual relationships we were bound to in our license agreements.

INVESTIGATION PROCESS

UCSD Libraries began looking for a solution to some of these problems in early 2002. We knew that a number of libraries were developing or had developed their own in-house electronic resources management systems (Johns

Hopkins, Harvard, and Pennsylvania State University among others). One of our sister campuses was also developing a system in-house. We had a presentation on their in-house system and its development and implementation and gave it serious consideration. Our main concerns were its lack of interoperability with our integrated library system and the need to provide local information technology support for both its implementation and ongoing maintenance. At this same time, our Information Technology Department was engaged in a number of other initiatives and there was a transition both in leadership and in staffing of that area. Initial estimates of the costs for us to look at outsourcing this operation were prohibitive. At this time, there were really no "off the shelf" solutions out there we could easily adopt that would meet all our needs.

BETA TESTING

It was at this same time that our integrated library system vendor Innovative Interfaces announced that they were working with five development partners to build an electronic resources management system (ERMS). This was in response to multiple requests from their customers for such a product that would be integrated into their existing integrated library system. UCSD Libraries have been Innovative users since 1986 and have often served as a beta test site for new releases of their software and for new modules. There are differing opinions about the advantages and disadvantages of beta testing. In general, it has been a positive experience for our library since we felt that we were often able to shape the development of a product. We anticipated that we would likely be "power users" of an electronic resources management system and wanted the ability to test its functionality for us and hopefully influence its future design. We expressed an interest in working with Innovative as a beta test site in early 2003 and were selected to implement the beta test in October 2003.

As a prelude to the beta test, staff members working with electronic resources and serials began developing a list of functional requirements that we hoped would be included in the product. Among them was the ability to address many of the issues identified in the beginning of this article: the ability to store title/package relationships in a more coherent way, the ability to store licensing information and push it out to users, and an integrated approach to managing the acquisitions and financial information related to electronic resources. In addition, we wanted a strong report-writing capability that would allow us to better evaluate the characteristics of our electronic resources and track them through their life cycle.

Early on, acquisitions staff recognized the importance of including all of the various stakeholders at the discussion table since it was becoming apparent that this would not exclusively be an acquisitions tool. Consequently, staff members from serials and electronic resources cataloging, public services, and collection development were added to the ERMS Beta Group. Though we all brought differing perspectives to the table, there were a number of commonalities that we identified.

At our first meeting, there was a spirited discussion on the need to follow standards in working with such a system. Standards did exist for some components of the ERMS (e.g., bibliographic records); however, for many of the data elements present in an electronic resources management system, there were no widely accepted standards. Since 2001, the Digital Library Federation's Electronic Resources Management Initiative (ERMI) had been working to develop a framework for electronic resources management systems discussion.[2] It had recently produced a draft of the data structure and functional requirements for systems.[3] One of our University of California colleagues had been active in the development of these documents and emphasized the importance of looking toward these as emerging standards for the development of electronic resources management systems. It has long been the practice of the University of California libraries to work towards and help develop standards that are interoperable within the University and within the library community at large. It was imperative that we work toward following the best practices available. We were hopeful that Innovative Interfaces would follow these guidelines as much as possible since they also had a representative at the discussions. As beta testers we also hoped to strongly influence their decision to follow these emerging guidelines.

We were able to participate in the beta test without any upgrades to our hardware. The installation of the client software was done by the vendor. Though we did not expect any immediate effect on system performance, we did monitor activity and response time after initial installation. One of the advantages of going with a product from our existing ILS vendor was the familiar look and feel of the interface. Although there were a number of new features and fields within records, the navigation of the system was identical to that of our cataloging, serials, and acquisitions modules. From an operational standpoint, very little training was required of our staff to begin working with the ERMS. However, from a conceptual perspective, we had to begin to think of things somewhat differently from how the other modules worked.

Our library entered the beta test with about eight other libraries, including two "stand-alone" users. Most of the libraries were academic libraries with similar electronic resources management needs. Early on during the beta testing, Innovative Interfaces had set up a listserv that allowed us to interact with each other and with Innovative. This was invaluable in our testing. Libraries were able to share experiences which Innovative closely monitored online. One of the greatest benefits of interacting with the other development partners and beta test libraries was the ability to share information (e.g., data fields and definitions), thus making the implementation go much more quickly. We didn't have to reinvent the wheel if one of the earlier users had developed working definitions that we could adapt.

TRAINING

Innovative conducted our training using Web-conferencing software. In general it worked well; however, it did require some hands-on use for all of us to become familiar with the software. Though the training had greatest benefit for those actually using the system we asked all the beta test group members to attend the training sessions so as to get a perspective of how the entire system worked. The broad representation of different areas on our Beta Test Group was very important as we provided feedback to Innovative as the product was being developed. Though public services staff often attached a value to certain information different from that of the acquisitions staff, there was a respect for the needs of all users. For example, some did not feel it was important to display relevant licensing information to the users, while others pointed out that it enabled us to meet our legal requirements. We often articulated this diversity of opinion back to Innovative. Cataloging members on the Beta Test Group were able to explain why certain things would and would not work in the system because of previous decisions that had been made about indexing, field display, and record structures. Working together, we were often able to find workaround solutions. Looking at the ERMS in a more holistic way enabled us to have a better understanding of how the system could work for us.

As indicated earlier, the navigation of the system was not the biggest challenge our users faced. The conceptual framework of the system, the entity relationships, and how those are expressed seemed to provide the biggest challenge. The further one was removed from the acquisitions and licensing process, the more difficult it was to grasp. Electronic resources don't usually fall into nice neat categories so we had to learn to deal with some of the ambiguities.

FEEDBACK TO THE VENDOR

Though we were only one of several beta test libraries, we were active in reporting issues to the vendor as we discovered them. We realized early on that we were going to be using the system a little differently than most of the other libraries. UCSD Libraries has had the good fortune of being able to catalog most of our electronic resources in house. In fact, our efforts were so successful that we were able to take on cataloging of the licensed shared content of the California Digital Libraries. Electronic resources are cataloged with the greatest degree of granularity possible then redistributed to other University of California libraries for loading into their online catalogs. Most libraries have had to look to publishers and commercial vendors such as Serials Solutions and TDNet to supply them with holdings and cataloging information for their electronic resources, in particular for journal content in aggregators. Therefore, it was important for Innovative to make this process a priority in their development of the ERMS. Though we are not able to benefit initially from these developments due to our present workflows, we are pleased that this functionality is present and anticipate that it will help us in the future.

ESTABLISHING PRIORITIES

Because we were only testing the product, we were reluctant to devote too much time to populating the database, yet we wanted to do enough work that we had a sense of the full functionality and utility of the product. Because part of the record structure was already in place (order records, bibliographic records, holdings records) we were able to do some population fairly easily and see how the record relationships worked. Some features, such as an automatic e-mail notification or "tickler file" was set up early in the process. We began to benefit from that feature immediately. It was so popular that other areas (serials and monographic acquisitions) wanted to try and use it for some of their workflows as well. Though we deliberately did not begin a large retrospective population of records, we decided to create and populate records to the fullest extent possible whenever we dealt with a resource in some way (renewal, licensing, trial, etc.). By the end of the beta test, we had a representative sample of records reflecting electronic journals, integrating resources, and databases. We deliberately decided to input only paid resources or those on trial. Our library has a locally developed portal so we do not immediately envision using the ERMS to provide access to free Web resources. However, we feel the potential is there to do so and we would evaluate it against existing alternatives for robustness, granularity, and functionality. Many libraries are relying upon their electronic resources management systems to provide them with their "A to Z lists" and other discovery tools.

We needed the ERMS to have report-writing capabilities that would allow us to assess both our collections and create administrative reports on a variety of issues. In general, the report-writing features rely on Boolean list creation and the export of data into a variety of formats. Delimited text data could be used within spreadsheets and other database management software. Our experience with "packaged" reports has been mixed, so initially we were looking for the ability to retrieve and manipulate data from as many categories as possible. As in any system, the data is only as useful as it is collected systematically. The ERMS offers a number of local fields that we were free to populate and name as we wished.

The current ERMS implementation group has deliberately waited to designate local fields until we have a greater sense of what our future needs will be.

As in many systems, the limitations on the number of fields available in a record force libraries to carefully choose how to populate locally defined fields to meet ever changing reporting needs.

The relationship of a library's link resolver to the electronic resources management system is often a consideration in some libraries. Some libraries want a high level of interoperability between the two. Because our library was relying on a combination of an in-house PURL server and a link resolver from another vendor, we did not have a "close coupling" between the ERMS and the link resolver. However, many libraries might wish to rely heavily upon the coverage or knowledge base that they have developed in relation to their link resolving technology to help populate their ERMS.

ERMS AS A DISCOVERY AND PUBLIC ACCESS TOOL

From its earliest inception, the ERMS was viewed as being a tool for the public. We wanted to display relevant information to our users whenever possible. As in all discussions of public displays, screen real estate is a hotly debated topic. Some catalogers want to display as much bibliographic information as they maintain (subject headings, notes, etc.) on the initial display. Some public service librarians are "minimalists" and want to display only the most essential information that could be digested by patrons. The display issue becomes even more problematic for those libraries that use a "single" record approach to cataloging print and electronic versions on the same record, because of the length of the bibliographic records as holdings information generally needs to display for both formats. Often there is information about access restrictions which also needs to display. One of the biggest challenges for UCSD libraries has been to arrive at a display format that is agreeable to all parties and that is understandable by the average user. Sometimes this means going to multiple layers of display. Complicating all of this is the evolving nature of integrated library systems as new software releases permit (and sometimes restrict) different public displays. Public display is very much a "work in progress" and will change as user needs change. User education also becomes important when certain license information is displayed to the public. For example, an authorized use described as "coursepack use allowed" may not be readily apparent to all users of the OPAC. Fortunately, our ERMS has a "non-public" side which can be viewed by library staff in its more "native" environment. Therefore, more detailed information on license terms, contact information, and financial information can be displayed for staff with various granularity of authorization levels.

ERMS AS A COLLECTION DEVELOPMENT TOOL

Another important user group for the ERMS is the library's subject bibliographers. As in most libraries, the expertise of bibliographers in using various components of an integrated library system will vary from user to user. Currently, bibliographers at UCSD have "read-only" privileges within the ERMS. Some libraries have chosen to empower their bibliographers with the ability to help populate the system by, among other things, writing general descriptions of the resource, assigning local subject headings, and updating information related to training and help pages for the resource. This can be highly successful, as the bibliographers are often the most knowledgeable of the resource and its capabilities and limitations. However, it can result in an uneven appearance and inconsistency in the data available from resource to resource. In cases where the ERMS is also used to manage free or open-access resources, the bibliographers play a key role in building the database and in maintaining it, since they are often acquired outside the traditional acquisitions process. The robustness of the ERMS as a collection development tool is closely tied to the robustness of the report generation features as well as to extent that records are populated with data that measure subject and content strengths.

DOWNSIDES OF BETA TESTING

Being a beta tester or early adaptor of a system has both its positive and negative aspects. During beta tests, the user documentation is often not fully developed (if it exists at all). Library staff must devote a considerable amount of time training themselves in navigating and using the system. Often one is working with a system that might change from one day to the next. It is not always readily apparent if a particular outcome is a result of user error or system design. At times it is often difficult to recreate a particular action so as to provide feedback to the vendor. Beta testing also carries with it the responsibility to report back to a vendor what seems to work and what doesn't. If a good beta testing infrastructure is in place (e.g., an online discussion, regular conference calls) this mechanism works well. Though there is a great deal of similarity in how libraries manage electronic resources, different libraries can have different experiences in how they use a system. Beta tests usually seek to have a wide representation of different types of libraries engaged in different activities using the system. As our library was not actively involved in batch loading information from third parties, the vendor was able to profit from the experience of other beta test libraries that were doing this extensively. Therefore we will be able to benefit from the changes made in response to the experience of these libraries. At times during a beta test, the product can take on different directions in response to feedback from libraries. Sometimes the vendor will make changes to the underlying architecture of the system. This did occur in our beta testing of the ERMS. Fortunately, the vendor was able to migrate all of the data into the new structure for us. Again, this is one of the reasons we were conservative about populating records during the beta test phase.

FUTURE CHALLENGES FOR THE ERMS

Currently most of the effort in electronic resources management systems development is focused on single library environments. Because so many electronic resources are purchased consortially, often with their costs being shared by a number of institutions, it is important the electronic resources management systems address consortial needs. Libraries within consortia need to be able to share information broadly with a great deal of granularity in authorizations level. Because member libraries often use disparate integrated library systems, it is difficult to share information within the contractual agreements that libraries have with ILS vendors. Consequently, there are often a number of "silos" where data resides that cannot be easily shared. Fortunately, the Digital Library Federation's ERMI has begun addressing some of the consortial issues in its most recent discussions.[4] Integrated library systems vendors are aware of the need for interoperability but are faced with the dilemma of protecting their intellectual property and market position while still trying to work with other vendors. The ability to exchange information electronically among these silos is also very much determined by emerging standards for data exchange. There are also discussions of sharing licensing information using various rights expression languages on the horizon such as Onix for Serials, METS, ODRL, XrML and others.[5] License information is particularly problematic because libraries license content on very customizable terms, thus making it an unlikely candidate for widespread distribution to many licensors. Future exchange of this data will depend upon the adoption of and promulgation of elements and definitions such as those being developed by the Digital Library Foundation's Electronic Resources Management Initiative. Because libraries have such immediate needs to manage this information, it is unlikely that many can wait until these are fully in place and adopted by all library systems vendors. As in the case of any library system, most libraries will undoubtedly migrate from one vendor to another at least once. It is imperative that data stored be in such a format that it can easily be migrated to another platform. Libraries are faced with the challenge of trying to create datasets while the standards are still emerging.

One of the other challenges we have identified is the ability to manage electronic resources that are monographic in nature within our Electronic Resources Management system. ERMS is very much designed to work with continuing resources, as there is a close interoperability with the serials control module. As more of our purchases are monographic in nature, it is unclear as to how robust the system will be in dealing with those. For example, some electronic resource aggregations such as *LION (Literature Online: the Home of English and American Literature on the World Wide Web)* contain many monographs and even individual literary works such as poems. The record structure with the ERMS is very much geared toward serial publications. However, as more monographic publications become digitized and as part of larger licensed collections, the electronic resources management systems will need to adapt to new formats and record structures. How well these systems are able to deal with different licensing terms for components within the same electronic resource still remains to be seen.

CONCLUSION

Being among the first to use a product has been both a challenging and rewarding experience. It has caused us to examine our existing workflows, rethink why we do things, and move to a much more distributed model of maintaining and sharing information related to electronic resources in a library environment.

NOTES

1. "California Digital Library: Overview and Mission," *http://www.cdlib.org/glance/overview.html* (Accessed 7 July 2004).
2. "DLF Electronic Resource Management Initiative," *http://www.diglib.org/standards/dlf-erm02.htm* (Accessed 13 July 2004).
3. "A Web Hub for Developing Administrative Metadata for Electronic Resource Management," *http://www.library.cornell.edu/cts/elicensestudy/* (Accessed 7 July 2004).
4. Adam Chandler, "Update on DLF Electronic Resources Management Initiative with Focus on XML Schema for e-Resources Licenses." Presentation, American Library Association Annual Conference, Orlando, FL, June 25, 2004.
5. Karen Coyle, "Rights Expression Languages: a Report for the Library of Congress." February 2004. *http://www.loc.gov/standards/Coylereport_final1single.pdf* (Accessed 13 July 2004).

Beginning to See the Light:
Developing a Discourse
for Electronic Resource Management

Jill Emery

SUMMARY. As the proliferation of electronic content continues, the need to get a better handle on how we communicate about the management of these resources has grown. In many instances, these processes and workflows have a basis in print resource workflow management. However, the discourse used to describe print resource management is not fully transferable to the management of electronic resources. With the rapid development of open-source software, ubiquitous acceptance of sophisticated integrated library systems, and emerging digital standards, new models for workflow and processing of electronic resources are emerging. Drawn from the discourse used in other disciplines, this paper explores ways to create a discourse of electronic resource management to better enable the development of a more universal management scheme for electronic resources. *[Article copies available for a fee from The Haworth Document Delivery Service: 1-800-HAWORTH. E-mail address: <docdelivery@haworthpress.com> Website: <http://www.HaworthPress.com> © 2005 by The Haworth Press, Inc. All rights reserved.]*

Jill Emery received her MLIS from the University of Texas at Austin and she is currently Director, Electronic Resources Program at the University of Houston Libraries, University of Houston, 114 University Libraries, Houston, TX 77204-2000 (E-mail: JEmery@uh.edu).

[Haworth co-indexing entry note]: "Beginning to See the Light: Developing a Discourse for Electronic Resource Management." Emery, Jill. Co-published simultaneously in *The Serials Librarian* (The Haworth Information Press, an imprint of The Haworth Press, Inc.) Vol. 47, No. 4, 2005, pp. 137-147; and: *Electronic Journal Management Systems: Experiences from the Field* (ed: Gary Ives) The Haworth Information Press, an imprint of The Haworth Press, Inc., 2005, pp. 137-147. Single or multiple copies of this article are available for a fee from The Haworth Document Delivery Service [1-800-HAWORTH, 9:00 a.m. - 5:00 p.m. (EST). E-mail address: docdelivery@haworthpress.com].

Digital Object Identifier: 10.1300/J123v47n04_13

KEYWORDS. Electronic resources, discourse, electronic resource management, e-material-to-order, e-material-to-stock, library network enterprise

OVERVIEW

At some point around the time that the Internet mileage dial was rolling from 1999 to 2000, a metaphoric shift occurred. We were no longer hurtling, willy-nilly, down Al Gore's "Information Super Highway"[1] as nomadic information seekers but found ourselves settling into William J. Mitchell's "e-topia."[2] E-global villages began to spring to life via remote satellite feeds, digital telecommunication networks, and a growing spread of instruments that feed off these advances in communication delivery. Each of us now requires not just a desktop computer but is also in need of a cell phone, a laptop, and a PDA in order to succeed in our electrified, globally connected society. Along with this metaphoric shift came a change in the attitude about information. We had crawled out of the gopher holes and were no longer chasing information down along a vast array of highways and byways but rather, we began to ask for tools that allowed us to download information into our numerous, informational handheld devices in a myriad of ways. Today, information has become a power source that must be consistently supplied and delivered through a multitude of channels that can be converted on a whim from one application to another.

For libraries, this has meant a shift from just gathering and collecting electronic resource access to developing new and better delivery mechanisms for these content streams through the use of cross-linking technologies and electronic journal management systems. Along with this, we have begun to create our own digital collections from our specialized print holdings and from the research performed by the faculty and researchers we serve. Our faculties and students are no longer content with a list of links on a rudimentary Web site and this has led to the development of dynamic Web pages, subject portals and personalized library Web space. Furthermore, the average library patron wants more immediacy to the access available, wants aggregated databases broken down into either journal title or book title level access points, and wants subject level access that makes search and retrieval intuitive. Libraries need to find ways to integrate the access to virtual collections with the static collections sitting on their shelves and be able to point to the utility of all material types. On top of all this comes the open access movement that further breaks down accessibility of resource access to the article and paper level.

By 2001, most libraries began some type of Web presence redesign process, and they began to investigating ways to quickly dump large bundles of electronic access points into our online public access catalogs, cross-reference linking between electronic resources, and to better organize our electronic access in ways that made finding access a no-brainer. Around this time, two other developments sprang up that added to the mobility of the scholarly information brokered by a library. OpenURL linking and metasearch mechanisms hit the library scene simultaneously. OpenURL linking gives a library the ability to provide resource discovery from one electronic resource to another electronic resource and metasearch tools provide the ability to search across a wide array of resources that may or may not have the same interface and platform structure.

Also in 2001, there was work beginning on each coast of the United States of America to develop a way to capture and serve out the grey literature being produced by faculty and researchers. Along with these developments, a more vocal call for open access to scholarly communication began to echo through the library literature and electronic discussion lists. This gave rise to the rapid developments of institutional repositories and the initial discussions and considerations of management of electronic resources at the article and paper level. As a developing trend that is slow to catch on with faculty and authors, institutional repositories are attempts to gather together the research and scholarly output produced by the faculty at a given institution. Lastly, special collections and archives now had the needed infrastructure and technological tools such as high definition scanners and more robust servers to start digitizing collections and making these resources available through the library's new Web presence.

The linear, transactional-based procedures typically used to move print material from the mailroom to the shelf are not fully adaptable to this new universe of knowledge. Some portions of these pre-existing procedures could work with electronic resources, but there are many more variables to take into account and to consider. Knowledge management has become needed to account for the various ways an electronic resource may be purchased, hosted, and supported. In addition, electronic resources require a sophisticated tracking mechanism to fully represent the decision making undertaken with each resource. There are also completely new avenues that have to be transgressed in making electronic access fully available to the end-user such as proxy server set-up and maintenance, resource target databases to support openURL tools, metadata needs for emerging, locally developed digital material, and the creation of institutional repositories. Lastly, once you have an electronic resource up and running, you cannot just walk away from it and let it serve its usefulness alone. No, you have to keep revisiting the access point to verify that it is still there and viable, that it is being visited regularly by patrons and that the patrons are able to fully utilize all the value-added mechanisms that it provides.

Suddenly, libraries around the globe are trying to figure out how to create a global village of information for their constituents and how to keep these information streams best supplied to their learning centers. However, it is also readily apparent that the tools needed to harness the energy of this information explosion are not available. So each library has begun to build ad hoc power grids to help monopolize on their capital expenditures and provide the most consistent streams of access available. Today, we find ourselves at a point in time where most libraries have a local, workable solution but there is still very much a desire to locate a more universal management scheme. This paper explores some of the ways to adopt the description of processes being employed in other disciplines and some of the concepts that are arising from information architecture discourse to try to provide newer ways to discuss electronic resource management.

THE FIVE COMPONENTS OF PURCHASED ELECTRONIC RESOURCE MANAGEMENT

There are five basic components of electronic resource management that all libraries grapple with when purchasing access to electronic resources. These are: acquisition, access provision, administration, support provision, and evaluation or monitoring of the access.[3] These components all require an interweaving of three basic business processes or systems management: transactional processes, knowledge management, and decision-support processes.[4] A transactional process is comprised of following the transactions undertaken to manage an electronic resource. Knowledge management can be defined as the handling of the explicit information known about an electronic resource and providing this knowledge out to all those who use or work with the electronic resource. Decision support should be understood as the compiling and warehousing of the decisions made about an electronic resource. Let's look at each of the five components of electronic resources individually.

Acquisition: Perhaps the most transactional-based process undertaken with electronic resources, this incorporates all of the initial processes one undertakes from running a trial of an electronic product, licensing the product, and payment of the product. In all of this, currently, only payment of the product is generally handled through an integrated library system. While payment may be the most recognizable process, it too has taken on a variable nature: do you pay through a subscription agent, through a 3rd party buying club, or through a consortia deal; is the resource provided by any type of statewide entity or funding mechanism? Payment is no longer the straightforward pay your subscription agent or publisher for access and oftentimes it takes numerous note field entries to fully explain how an item is accounted for financially. Numerous institutions have also created licensing databases to spell out the terms and conditions of licensed access which make up a solid knowledge management component that did not exist with print material. These databases are either designed in MS Access or SQL with some sort of ColdFusion interface to an Intranet/Internet environment. Some libraries have set up trial tracking mechanisms or a decision-making database to review products but most libraries manage the trial of an electronic resource through e-mail exchanges, a collection management committee that still meets in person, and subject librarian expertise.

Access Provision: A multitude of transactional and decision-making processes are employed with this component. This step is sometimes very linear, you pay a company for access and then you receive the provision of access with the delivery of a URL. However, most of the time, this is a complicated procedure that involves IP verification, working between a subscription agent, a platform provider, and a publisher to insure access has indeed been paid for and obtaining the correct codes to allow for access. Then there are also the internal set-up mechanisms that allow for remote access either in other campus buildings or through some remote log-in capability. This usually involves working through at least two different administrative interfaces, one locally and one remotely, to make sure access has been established correctly.

Administration: Primarily comprised of tracking the decision-making processes undertaken with the resource, this component also requires support from a knowledge management tool to track the movement of access. This step is comprised of validating that the content purchased is being made available, adding resources to whatever Web entities the library provides as well as adding resources into the online public access catalog. There is always some follow-up in relation to administration due to a change in content, platform provider, new server additions, or new URL implementation. Lastly, this component takes into account the set-up preferences required by each library to provide an individual look and feel to the access provided by the library.

Service Provision: With this step, the primary need is for a knowledge management tool to supply support contact information. Secondly, a decision-making tracking system could be employed to manage and record service histories of access. This is following up with any problems that your end-users encounter. There are also scheduled maintenance downtimes to log and track and service problems that may need to be addressed during the renewal period. Sometimes service provision is as simple as showing someone how to navigate and use the resource or even more removed how to navigate from their computing device to the resource.

Evaluation/Monitoring: Again, this component is primarily supported by a knowledge management tool and a decision-support tool. This is where usage statistics come into play. A look at how much use a resource is getting, how the resource is being used in correlation to other electronic resources, where the heaviest use happens within a resource is also noted. Close monitoring of the use of a resource can indicate educational needs to be addressed through instruction sessions, the need to further market access to this resource to your user community as a whole, and/or a fundamental problem with the resource that may need to be addressed by the company.

While it is easy to delineate between these five components, each segment does feed back into one another and thus the management of electronic resources is more of a cyclical process than a flat linear procedure. On top of this, no two electronic resource providers work or manage their resources in quite the same ways. We can state that almost all electronic resources entail looking at these five components but how these five components may relate to one another varies from resource to resource and provider to provider. This makes creating a systematic workflow that much more difficult.

E-MATERIAL-TO-ORDER

In the preface to his book *Internet-Based Workflow Management: Towards a Semantic Web*, Dan Marinescu writes: "There are two aspects of workflow management: one covers the understanding of the underlying process; the other aspect covers the infrastructure of handing individual cases."[5] This statement seems extremely applicable to electronic resource management. The basic tenants or components that have been outlined above provide the underlying process that a library goes through when purchasing access to an electronic resource; however, each of these resources is slightly different from the one before and the one after, so whatever workflow is developed must also take into consideration the individuality of each resource to be processed. In many ways, we should look at the management of electronic resources as an on-demand process much like Dell Computing goes through to assemble an online computer order. In this case, there exists the same basic situation of an order being placed, an order being assembled, and then the goods delivered to the end-user. Processing of electronic resources follows this same scheme. A subject librarian/collection management committee requests an electronic resource, acquisition of the resource occurs, access provision is completed, administration of the resource is undertaken, service provision occurs when needed and a monthly, quarterly, or annual evaluation of the resource should occur. How each of these components is handled in regards to a single electronic resource may differ but the fundamental underlying process is the same. Some resources will take longer to process than others. Some electronic resources will require more attention or more detail than others; however, in the end result, access to the electronic product is achieved.

This is a fundamental shift in our thinking of processing material in a library. We are accustomed to a set, rote, transactional procedure that can basically be accomplished in the much same manner each time for each entity that is the same such as a print journal or a print book. However, electronic resources require us to take both a systematic approach of dealing with the same five components and an automatic approach where these five components may or may not fit together in the same way each time and we may have to add or subtract processes on the fly. Part of the reason why there has been such a struggle to develop an electronic resource management tool is because what is needed is a tool that provides us with the ability to perform transaction processing, house-needed knowledge management elements, and provide room for decision support mechanisms. The merger of these three information systems requires a complete redesign or reconceptualization of what an integrated library system was originally intended for and there are developments underway by all of the major integrated library system vendors to develop tools that make attempts to fulfill all of these needs. However, this type of restructuring of a full-fledged integrated system requires time and thoughtful consideration. The resulting mechanism should not rely too heavily on old standards and practices but allow for the development of new standards and procedures to be created and utilized.

Due to the fact that most libraries have been developing management tools in an ad hoc fashion to help manage electronic resources, there is no standardization in place for the locally developed systems that have been created. The Web Hub for Developing Administrative Metadata for Electronic Resource Management, *http://www.library.cornell.edu/cts/elicensestudy/home.html,*[6] is a tremendously important undertaking. Once standardization of the metadata is in place, open-source tools could be developed outside of integrated library systems that would allow a library to pull together locally developed management structures into a unified structure of purchased electronic resource management.

E-MATERIAL-TO-STOCK

Libraries are no longer just purchasing electronic resources. In many cases, libraries are developing some type of digital or electronic collection either from their specialized collection areas, electronic theses/dissertations, institutional or city archives or with the development of an institutional repository to capture the research of faculty and staff.[7] The developments of these e-collections are often undertaken by either a specialized task force at the library or by the personnel of the special collections/archives realm. Sometimes, these e-collections are designed or developed in partnership with the local community which they serve and sometimes, these digital collections are created solely from the library. There are many unknowns in the development of these local e-collections. Libraries are attempting to utilize standards, metadata, and systems that will allow for scalability of these local products to technologies of the future but the stability and mobility of these new electronic resources have yet to stand the test of time.[8]

In this role, the library is becoming the producer of the electronic resource and the general underlying concept is that these collections will be the virtual representation of the book shelves. In other words, the library is producing content to stock their virtual libraries in an attempt to meet future needs and demands as opposed to just reacting to present needs and requests from their constituents. Libraries have always been involved in the warehousing or collection of the universe of knowledge, so this concept is not necessarily all that novel on the surface. The novelty of this practice comes primarily in relation to the development of institutional repositories. Institutional repositories are unique in that we are attempting to provide access to a more granular level of material than we have previously. We are beginning to see the deconstruction of the delivery vessel of the journal with the advent of open access paradigms.

Open access discourse is by and large held at the article/paper level. For almost a decade now, we've lived with the collection and management of the electronic pre-print. Pre-prints are articles/papers that have yet to be published in a peer-reviewed, impact-gauged journal. Most recently, we've seen a dramatic rise in the ability for authors to form post-print e-collections. These are articles/papers that are to be published in a journal but the publisher is now allowing the author the ability to self-archive their research/work as long as it is the article submitted for publication and not the final copy that has been published. In order to fully take advantage of this ability to self-archive, libraries and institutions are creating repositories where faculty can deposit their articles/papers for retrieval. Suddenly, the library/institution is taking on the role of becoming an aggregator and developing an aggregated database of locally produced content. This is a new role for the library to play and one that will eventually lead to new manners of discourse and a potentially major shift in scholarly dissemination that can not be foreseen at this time.

LIBRARY ENTERPRISE NETWORK

In his book *The Internet Galaxy*, Manuel Castells defines e-business as a network enterprise:

> Thus, the network enterprise is neither a network of enterprises nor an intra-firm, networked organization. Rather, it is a lean agency of economic activity, built around specific business projects, which are enacted by networks of various composition and origin: *the network is the enterprise*. While the firm continues to be the unit of accumulation of capital, property rights (usually), and strategic management, business practice is performed by *ad hoc* networks. These networks have the flexibility and adaptability required by a global economy subjected to relentless technological innovation and stimulated by rapidly changing demand.[9]

In relation to electronic resources, this is what libraries are becoming: a library enterprise network where the work needed to acquire/develop, process, and make electronic resources accessible is performed by ad hoc networks or partnerships. A network node is more closely developed between subject librarians and faculty/researchers to help delineate what electronic resources are needed on demand or to order, and what electronic resources should be stocked or deposited into the institutional repository. Instruction librarians are working with subject librarians and faculty/researchers to try to provide relevant information literacy in regards to the utilized electronic resources in a given discipline. Any librarian involved in collection development has created some type of network node with the publishers and vendors who provide electronic resources. In turn, the vendors have developed a close network with the publishers as well as a network back to the librarians. In addition, electronic resources/serials librarians have developed network models with the electronic resource management tool providers as well. These librarians in turn have networks established with the subject librarians and another network established with the systems librarians who develop and manage the technological constructs into which we house our electronic resource management tools. These networks nodes are constantly changing and realigning, coming together as task forces to work on specific projects and being disbanded and reformed as one project is completed and another one develops. [10]

The management of electronic resources requires a more fluid and dynamic workflow and while single points of service are starting junctures, service provision in relation to electronic material is a broader scope than just one or two people within a library organization. The fundamental comprehension of how electronic resources are created, marketed, and provided is needed by a larger portion of the library organization than what was previously needed with print-focused collections. Most importantly to consider here is that in order to achieve successful management of electronic resources in any one given place or instance, we must work directly and closely with people and groups outside the given sphere of the library. It is impossible to provide the fullest possible service in relation to electronic resources management and maintain an insular, library-only point of view.

CONCLUSION: I COULD BE WRONG/I COULD BE RIGHT

This paper has made an attempt to explore concepts from other disciplines to help develop a better discourse for electronic resource management. We should recognize that the purchase and provision of electronic resources requires us to develop three systematic processing approaches: transactional, knowledge management and decision support. With this comprehension, we should be better able to develop standardized management tools that lead to a more streamlined workflow and arrangement of processing of electronic resources. Furthermore, we begin to realize that there exist components to the purchasing of electronic resource management that occur but are not necessarily consistent from any one given resource to another and that each of these components requires us to employ all three of the systematic processing approaches outlined.

There is a delineation made between purchased electronic resources or resources obtained on-demand for our constituents and the electronic resources that are developed in-house and stocked in the virtual library for future discovery and use. In relation to the stocked electronic resources we are taking on a management role at the article/paper level and attempting to develop institution-based or subject-based aggregated collections of electronic articles/papers. The future development of this area in libraries could have further discourse development.

Lastly, we need to reconceptualize our internal management to one that is more of a networking scheme and embrace the concept of ad hoc processing, development, and support of electronic resources. By recognizing there are various nodes of interaction that occur in regards to electronic resource management and access, we realize that management of electronic resources is not something that can occur within just task-specific or format-specific realms.[11] Lastly, the realization should be made that our partnerships in regards to the management of electronic material are not just local interactions but also interactions with parties beyond the scope of the physical library realm.

Despite the predictions that libraries would be left choking on the dust as our constituents zoomed off down the information super highway, libraries have made a place for themselves in e-topia. Libraries continue to serve as the information epicenters for our learning centers. We've done well developing rudimentary information grids to supply needed information to our constituents and we need to focus on how to continue to further refine and develop our provision to electronic resources. Through the adoption of more flexible and adaptable organizational structures and the development of standards for electronic resource management we will be able to meet the growing needs of those we serve. Otherwise, we may end up in the dark, marginalized area of the e-global village, wondering how we fell off the information grids we helped create.

NOTES

1. Mitchell Kapor, "Where Is the Digital Highway Really Heading?," *Wired Magazine*, July/Aug 1993.

2. William J. Mitchell, *e-topia: Urban Life, Jim–But Not As We Know It* (Cambridge: MIT Press, 2000).

3. Stuart D. Lee, *Electronic Collection Development: A Practical Guide* (New York: Neal-Schuman Publishers Inc., 2002).

4. Wil van der Aalst and Kees van Hee, *Workflow Management: Models, Methods, and Systems* (Cambridge: MIT Press, 2002).

5. Dan C. Marinescu, *Internet-Based Workflow Management* (New York: John Wiley & Sons, 2002).

6. *http://www.library.cornell.edu/cts/elicensestudy/home.html* Viewed 8/1/2004.

7. Marilyn Deegan and Simon Tanner, *Digital Futures: Strategies for the Information Age* (New York: Neal-Schuman Publishers, Inc., 2002).

8. Mark Ware Consulting Ltd, *Publisher and Library/Learning Solutions (PAALS) Pathfinder Research on Web-Based Repositories: FINAL REPORT*, January 2004 *http://www.palsgroup.org.uk/palsweb/palsweb.nsf/08c43ce800a9c67cd80256e370051e88a/ $FILE/PALS%20report%20on%20Institutional%20Repositories.pdf* Viewed 7/20/2004.

9. Manuel Castells, *The Internet Galaxy: Reflections on the Internet, Business, and Society* (Oxford: Oxford University Press, 2001).

10. Jason Charvat, *Project Management Nation: Tools, Techniques, and Goals for the New and Practicing IT Manager* (New York: John Wiley & Sons, 2002).

11. Rachael K. Anderson, "The Impact of Digital Libraries on Library Staffing and Education," in *Development of Digital Libraries: An American Perspective*, ed. Deanna B. Marcum (Westport: Greenwood Press, 2001).

Index

A-to-Z and LinkSource (EBSCO), 42-54
A-to-Z, 42-52
  background and historical
    perspectives, 45-47
  customer support issues, 47-48
  implementation-related issues,
    48-52
    branding, 48-49
    customization, 48
    proxy access, 52
    title list maintenance, 50-52
    usage reports, 52
  LinkSource, 52-53
  overviews and summaries, 42-45
  system descriptions, 45-47
Access-related issues, 80-82,141
Acquisition-related issues, 140-141
Active Server Pages (ASP), 81
Adams, B., 29
Administrative functions, 97-98
AISTI (Alliance for Innovation in
    Science and Technology),
    11-13
Alan, R., 1-2,17-25
ARL (Association of Research
    Libraries), 20,56-57,73
ASP (Active Server Pages), 81
Association of Research Libraries
    (ARL), 20,56-57,73

Background and historical
    perspectives. *See also under*
    individual topics
A-to-Z and LinkSource (EBSCO),
    45-47

beta testing and implementation
    perspectives, 126-127
customized systems, 90-92
discourse development processes,
    138-140
evolutionary approaches, 56-59
master serials lists, 5-6
SFX and Serials Solutions, 72-
    74,80
  Texas A&M University
    Libraries experiences, 72-74
  University of Wisconsin-La
    Crosse (Murphy Library)
    experiences, 80
TDNet, 28-29,36
  Boise State University
    (Albertsons Library)
    experiences, 28-29
  University of South Carolina
    (Thomas Cooper Library)
    experiences, 36
transition-related perspectives
    (in-house to in-house/vendor
    systems), 18
workflow-related perspectives,
    104-105
Beta testing and implementation
    perspectives, 125-136
  background and historical
    perspectives, 126-127
  beta testing processes, 129-131
  collection development issues,
    133-134
  discovery tools, 133
  feedback-to-vendor issues, 131-132
  functional needs identification,
    127-128

future perspectives, 135-136
investigation processes, 128-129
negative factors, 134
overviews and summaries,
    125-126
priorities identification, 132-133
public access tools, 133
reference resources, 136
training-related issues, 131
Bibliographies. *See* Reference
    resources
Birrell, A., 33
Boise State University (Albertsons
    Library) experiences, 27-34
Branding-related issues, 48-49
Breeding, M., 23-24
Brown, C., 105
Brown, J.F., 1-2,89-102

California Digital Library (CDL),
    127,131-132
Castells, M., 144-145
CDL (California Digital Library),
    127,131-132
Chandler, A., 106
ColdFusion, 20,140-141
Cole, J., 2
Collection development issues,
    133-134
Content descriptions, 92-97
Cooper, P.S., 1-2,27-34
Crosse, G., 1-2
Crum, J., 1-2,103-124
Customer support issues, 47-48
Customized systems, 89-102
    A-to-Z and LinkSource (EBSCO),
        48
    background and historical
        perspectives, 90-92
    database development, 92-100
        administrative functions, 97-98
        content descriptions, 92-97
        overviews and summaries, 92
        public functions, 98-100

staff roles and responsibilities,
    100
future perspectives, 101-102
multi-library perspectives, 89-102
need for, 91-92
overviews and summaries, 89-90
reference resources, 102

Database development, 92-100
    administrative functions, 97-98
    content descriptions, 92-97
    overviews and summaries, 92
    public functions, 98-100
    staff roles and responsibilities, 100
DataswetsConnect, 92-93
Davis, T., 1-2,103-124
Dell Computing, 142
Design and layout issues, 6-13
Digital Library Federation (DLF), 18,
    24,105,123,130-131
Discourse development processes,
    137-147
    background and historical
        perspectives, 138-140
    e-material-to-order, 142-143
    e-material-to-stock, 143-144
    future perspectives, 145-146
    library enterprise networks,
        144-145
    linear transactional procedures,
        139-140
    overviews and summaries, 137-140
    purchased ERM components,
        140-142
        access provision, 141
        acquisition, 140-141
        evaluation and monitoring,
            141-142
        overviews and summaries, 140
        service provision, 141
    reference resources, 146-147
Discovery tools, 133
DLF (Digital Library Federation), 18,
    24,105,123,130-131

Duranceau, E.F., 37-38
Dylan, B., 33
Dynix Horizon, 90-92

E-global villages concept, 138,146
E-material-to-order, 142-143
E-material-to-stock, 143-144
E-topia concept, 138
EBSCO (A-to-Z and LinkSource),
  45-54
Eddings, D., 28
EISSN (electronic version)
  information, 114
Electronic holdings management,
  113-116
Electronic journal management system
  topics. *See also under*
  individual topics
A-to-Z and LinkSource (EBSCO),
  42-54
beta testing and implementation
  perspectives, 125-136
customized systems, 89-102
discourse development processes,
  137-147
evolutionary approaches, 55-70
master serials lists, 3-15
overviews and summaries, 1-2
SFX and Serials Solutions, 71-88
  Texas A&M University
    Libraries experiences, 71-78
  University of Wisconsin-La
    Crosse (Murphy Library)
    experiences, 79-88
TDNet, 27-42
  Boise State University
    (Albertsons Library)
    experiences, 27-34
  University of South Carolina
    (Thomas Cooper Library)
    experiences, 35-42
transition-related perspectives (in-
  house to in-house/vendor
  systems), 17-25

workflow-related perspectives, 103-
  124
Electronic Resource Licensing Center
  (ERLIC), 17-25
Electronic Resource Management
  Initiative (ERMI),
  18,24,106,123,130-131
Electronic Resource Management
  (Innovative Interfaces, Inc.),
  103-124
Elsevier ScienceDirect, 20,58-59
Emery, J., 2,137-147
Enterprise networks, 144-145
ERLIC (Electronic Resource Licensing
  Center), 17-25
ERM (electronic resource management)/
  journal management system
  topics. *See also under*
  individual topics
A-to-Z and LinkSource (EBSCO),
  42-54
beta testing and implementation
  perspectives, 125-136
customized systems, 89-102
discourse development processes,
  137-147
evolutionary approaches, 55-70
master serials lists, 3-15
overviews and summaries, 1-2
SFX and Serials Solutions, 71-88
  Texas A&M University
    Libraries experiences, 71-78
  University of Wisconsin-La
    Crosse (Murphy Library)
    experiences, 79-88
TDNet, 27-42
  Boise State University
    (Albertsons Library)
    experiences, 27-34
  University of South Carolina
    (Thomas Cooper Library)
    experiences, 35-42
transition-related perspectives
  (in-house to in-house/vendor
  systems), 17-25

workflow-related perspectives,
103-124
ERMI (Electronic Resource
Management Initiative),
18,24,106,123,130-131
Evaluation and monitoring issues,
141-142
Evolutionary approaches, 55-70
background and historical
perspectives, 56-59
ERM tools, 59-67
database link pages, 61
e-journal pages, 62-63
library Websites, 59
OPACs, 59-60
overviews and summaries, 59
subject guides, 61-62
future perspectives, 67-70
opportunities and challenges, 63
overviews and summaries, 55-57
preparation- and planning-related
issues, 67-69
print-to-electronic transitions,
57-59
reference resources, 70
staffing strategies, 66-69
vendor systems, 63-66
Extenza gateway, 95-97
EZProxy, 32-33

Feedback-to-vendor issues, 131-132
FileMaker Pro and Lasso systems,
91-92
Functional needs identification,
127-128
Fundamental topics. *See* Overviews
and summaries
Future perspectives. *See also under
individual topics*
beta testing and implementation
perspectives, 135-136
customized systems, 101-102
evolutionary approaches, 67-70
master serials lists, 13-15

SFX and Serials Solutions,
77-78,86-88
Texas A&M University
Libraries experiences, 77-78
University of Wisconsin-La
Crosse (Murphy Library)
experiences, 86-88
TDNet, 33-34,41-42
Boise State University
(Albertsons Library)
experiences, 33-34
University of South Carolina
(Thomas Cooper Library)
experiences, 41-42
transition-related perspectives
(in-house to in-house/vendor
systems), 23-24
workflow-related perspectives, 123

Gardner, S., 105
Gerhard, K.H., 105
Gore, A., 138
Gorman, M., 29,33

Harrell, J., 2
Harvell, T.A., 1-2,125-136
HighWire gateway, 95-97
Historical perspectives. *See*
Background and historical
perspectives
Holdings management, 113-116
Holman, J.S., 79-88

ILS (integrated library system)
integration issues, 4-6,
63-68,81-83,90-91
Implementation-related issues. *See
also under individual topics*
A-to-Z and LinkSource (EBSCO),
48-52
beta testing, 125-136

SFX and Serials Solutions,
74-78,82-84
Texas A&M University
Libraries experiences, 74-78
University of Wisconsin-
La Crosse (Murphy Library)
experiences, 82-84
TDNet, 31-34,37-41
Boise State University
(Albertsons Library)
experiences, 31-34
University of South Carolina
(Thomas Cooper Library)
experiences, 37-41
In-house to in-house/vendor system
transitions, 17-25
Ingenta gateway, 95-97
Innovative Interfaces, Inc. (Electronic
Resource Management),
103-124
Integrated library system (ILS)
integration issues, 4-6,
63-68,81-83,90-91
Introductory topics. *See* Overviews and
summaries
Investigation processes, 128-129
IP recognition van verification,
95-97,110,141
ISSN-related issues, 4-9,62-65,
83-86,114
Ives, G., 1-2,71-78

Jasper, R.P., 1-2,55-70
Jewell, T., 105
JournalWebSite, 29-30
JSTOR, 8,128
JWP (Joint Working Party) on the
Exchange of Serials
Subscription Information, 18

Kawasaki, J.L., 1-15

Lasso and FileMaker Pro systems,
91-92
Layout and design issues, 6-13
LC classification, 9
Lester, D., 1-2,27-34
Lexis-Nexis, 75
Library enterprise networks, 144-145
Library-specific experiences. *See also
under individual topics*
Boise State University (Albertsons
Library), 27-34
Montana State University (Renne
Library), 3-15
Ohio State University Libraries,
103-124
Oregon Health & Science
University Library, 103-124
Pennsylvania State University
College of Medicine
(George T. Harrell Library),
43-54
Pennsylvania State University
(Paterno Library), 17-25
Texas A&M University Libraries,
71-78
University of California (San
Diego) Libraries, 125-136
University of South Carolina
(Thomas Cooper Library),
35-42
University of Southern California
multiple library system,
89-102
University of Wisconsin-La Crosse
(Murphy Library), 79-88
Wayne State University Libraries,
55-70
Licensing-related issues, 110-112
Linear transactional procedures,
139-140
Lingle, V.A., 1-2,43-54
LinkSource (EBSCO), 45-54
Loading-related issues, 113-116

Macintosh FileMaker Pro and Lasso
    systems, 91-92
MARC-formatted bibliographic
    records, 85,105-108,114,128
Marinescu, D., 142-143
Markwith, M., 37-38
Marshall, S.P., 1-15
Master serials lists, 3-15
    background and historical
        perspectives, 5-6
    future perspectives, 13-15
    overviews and summaries, 3-5
    solution processes, 6-16
        designs and layouts, 6-13
        Microsoft Excel, 3-16
        MySQL, 6-16
        overviews and summaries, 6
McCracken, P., 29
McMullen, K., 1-2,35-42
Meagher, E., 105
MetaLib, 80
Microsoft products, 19-20,74-75,
    81,117,140-141
    Microsoft Access, 19-20,81,
        140-141
    Microsoft ASP (Active Server
        Pages), 81
    Microsoft Excel, 3-16
    Microsoft SQL, 74-75,117,140-141
Migration-related issues, 88
Mitchell, W.J., 138
Monitoring and evaluation issues,
    141-142
Montana State University (Renne
    Library) experiences, 3-15
Multi-library perspectives, 89-102
MUSE. *See* Project MUSE
MySQL, 6-16,91-92

NASIG (North American Serials
    Interest Group), 110-111
Nelson, J.L., 1-2,89-102
NISO (National Information Standards
    Organization), 18,41,106

Ohio State University Libraries
    experiences, 103-124
OpenURLs and OpenURL resolvers,
    33-39,52-53,123,139-140
Oregon Health & Science University
    Library experiences, 103-124
Overviews and summaries. *See also
    under individual topics*
    A-to-Z and LinkSource (EBSCO),
        42-45
    beta testing and implementation
        perspectives, 125-126
    customized systems, 89-90
    discourse development processes,
        137-140
    evolutionary approaches, 55-57
    of fundamental concepts, 1-2
    master serials lists, 3-5
    SFX and Serials Solutions, 71,
        79-80
        Texas A&M University
            Libraries experiences, 71
        University of Wisconsin-
            La Crosse (Murphy Library)
            experiences, 79-80
    TDNet, 17-18,27-28
        Boise State University
            (Albertsons Library)
            experiences, 27-28
        University of South Carolina
            (Thomas Cooper Library)
            experiences, 35-36
    Transition-related perspectives
        (in-house to in-house/vendor
        systems), 17-18
    workflow-related perspectives,
        103-104
Ovid, 92-95

Pennsylvania State University College
    of Medicine (George T.
    Harrell Library) experiences,
    43-54

Pennsylvania State University (Paterno Library) experiences, 17-25
PHP manipulation, 91-92,98-100
Pierce, L., 105
Pre-prints (electronic), 144
Preparation- and planning-related issues, 67-69
Presentation-related issues, 117-121
Print-to-electronic transitions, 57-59
Priorities identification, 132-133
Project MUSE, 10,128
ProQuest, 20,29,75
Proxy access, 52
Public access tools, 133
Public functions, 98-100
Purchased ERM components, 140-142
    access provision, 141
    acquisition, 140-141
    evaluation and monitoring, 141-142
    overviews and summaries, 140
    service provision, 141
Purchasing-related issues, 112-113

Ramirez, R., 110-111
Readings. *See* Reference resources
Record structures, 107-108
Reference resources, 146-147. *See also under individual topics*
    beta testing and implementation perspectives, 136
    customized systems, 102
    discourse development processes, 146-147
    evolutionary approaches, 70
    SFX and Serials Solutions, 88
    TDNet, 34,42
    Boise State University (Albertsons Library) experiences, 34
    University of South Carolina (Thomas Cooper Library) experiences, 42

transition-related perspectives (in-house to in-house/vendor systems), 24
    workflow-related perspectives, 123-124
Reporting-related issues, 116-117
Robbins, S., 105
Roberts, G., 81

Scholar's Portal, 94-95
ScienceDirect (Elsevier), 20
Selection-related issues, 29-31, 36-37,108-110
Semantic Web concept, 142-143
Serials Solutions, 29-30
Service provision issues, 141
SFX and Serials Solutions, 55-88, 94-95
    Texas A&M University Libraries experiences, 71-78
    background and historical perspectives, 72-74
    future perspectives, 77-78
    implementation-related issues, 74-78
    overviews and summaries, 71
    University of Wisconsin-La Crosse (Murphy Library) experiences, 79-88
    access-related issues, 80-82
    background and historical perspectives, 80
    future perspectives, 86-88
    implementation-related issues, 82-84
    migration-related issues, 88
    overviews and summaries, 79-80
    reference resources, 88
    Wayne State University Library System experiences, 55-70
Sheble, L., 1-2,55-70
SIRSI Unicorn, 20-25
Sitko, M., 37-38
Solution processes, 6-16

Staffing strategies, 66-69,100
Standards-related issues, 18,41,106
Stat!Ref, 94-95
Strader, C.R., 1-2,103-124
Summary topics. *See* Overviews and
 summaries
Swets Information Service
 (DataswetsConnect), 92-93
System descriptions, 45-47
Szczyrbach, G., 105
Szilvassy, J., 33

TDNet, 27-42
 Boise State University (Albertsons
  Library) experiences, 27-34
 background and historical
  perspectives, 28-29
 comparisons charts, 30
 future perspectives, 33-34
 implementation-related
  perspectives, 31-34
 overviews and summaries, 27-28
 reference resources, 34
 selection-related perspectives,
  29-31
 University of South Carolina
  (Thomas Cooper Library)
  experiences, 35-42
 background and historical
  perspectives, 36
 future perspectives, 41-42
 implementation-related issues,
  37-41
 overviews and summaries, 35-36
 reference resources, 42
 selection-related issues, 36-37
Teaster, G., 110-111
Texas A&M University Libraries
 experiences, 71-78
Title list maintenance, 50-52
Training-related issues, 131
Transition-related perspectives (in-
 house to in-house/vendor
 systems), 17-25

background and historical
 perspectives, 18
ERLIC (Electronic Resource
 Licensing Center)
 development, 19-23
future perspectives, 23-24
limiting factors, 20-21
overviews and summaries, 17-18
reference resources, 24
standards development, 18
vendor solution integration and
 migration issues, 22-23
Troubleshooting issues, 121-123
Tull, L., 1-2,103-124

University of California (San Diego)
 Libraries experiences,
 125-136
University of South Carolina (Thomas
 Cooper Library) experiences,
 35-42
University of Southern California
 multiple library system
 experiences, 89-102
University of Wisconsin-La Crosse
 (Murphy Library)
 experiences, 79-88
Updating-related issues, 115-116
URL links, 107,117-121
Usage reports, 52
User support, 117-123

Wayne State University Libraries
 experiences, 55-70,103-124
Web Hub for Developing
 Administrative Metadata for
 Electronic Resource
 Management, 143
Wilmott, D., 1-2,35-42
Wineburgh-Freed, M., 1-2,89-102
Workflow-related perspectives,
 103-124

background and historical
    perspectives, 104-105
electronic holdings management,
    113-116
    loading-related issues, 113-116
    maintenance issues, 114-115
    updating-related issues, 115-116
future perspectives, 123
licensing-related issues, 110-112
overviews and summaries, 103-104
purchasing-related issues, 112-113
record structures, 107-108

reference resources, 123-124
reporting-related issues, 116-117
selection-related issues, 108-110
system development, 105-107
user support, 117-123
    presentation-related issues,
    117-121
    troubleshooting issues, 121-123

Z39.50 issues, 85